MODERN WORLD NATIONS

MODERN WORLD NATIONS

Pakistan

Samuel Willard Crompton
Holyoke Community College

Series Consulting Editor
Charles F. Gritzner
South Dakota State University

CHELSEA HOUSE
P U B L I S H E R S
A Haights Cross Communications ✦ Company
Philadelphia

Frontispiece: Flag of Pakistan

Cover: Pakistan is a land of many contrasts. Its landscape varies from the steep mountains of the Karakoram Range to the arid deserts of Baluchistan.

CHELSEA HOUSE PUBLISHERS

VP, NEW PRODUCT DEVELOPMENT Sally Cheney
DIRECTOR OF PRODUCTION Kim Shinners
CREATIVE MANAGER Takeshi Takahashi
MANUFACTURING MANAGER Diann Grasse

Staff for PAKISTAN

EDITOR Lee Marcott
PRODUCTION EDITOR Jaimie Winkler
PICTURE RESEARCHER Pat Holl
COVER AND SERIES DESIGNER Takeshi Takahashi
LAYOUT 21st Century Publishing and Communications, Inc.

A Haights Cross Communications ⚑ Company

http://www.chelseahouse.com

First Printing

1 3 5 7 9 8 6 4 2

Library of Congress Cataloging-in-Publication Data

Crompton, Samuel Willard.
   Pakistan / Samuel Willard Crompton.
      p. cm.—(Modern world nations)
Includes index.
Summary: Describes the history, geography, government, economy, people, and culture of Pakistan.
   ISBN 0-7910-7098-0
   1. Pakistan—Juvenile literature. [1. Pakistan.] I. Title. II. Series.
DS376.9 .C76 2002
954.91—dc21

                                                                        2002007348

Table of Contents

Pakistan

The 40-mile-long road known as the Khyber Pass has long been the route used for travelers between Pakistan and Afghanistan, as well as conquerors seeking to subdue the natives of the region.

CHAPTER 1

Pakistan, The Land of the Pure

What is this life of yours, tell me its mystery—
Trampled in dust is your ages-old history!
Deep in that dust has been smothered your flame—
Wake, and hear dawn its high summons proclaim!

—Poems from Muhammad Iqbal

Muhammad Iqbal was an Indian poet inspired with a vision of a new world, one informed both by the ages-old history of the Indian subcontinent and by Islam, the faith of the Prophet Muhammad. In numerous poems, Iqbal urged his fellow Muslims to rise and become a great force in the world, as was their destiny.

One of Iqbal's poems was "To the Panjab Peasant:"

What is this life of yours, tell me its mystery—
Trampled in dust is your ages-old history!
Deep in that dust has been smothered your flame—
Wake, and hear dawn its high summons proclaim!
Creatures of dust from the soil may draw bread:
Not in that darkness is Life's river fed!
Base will his metal be held, who on earth
Put not to trial his innermost worth!
Break all the idols of tribe and of caste,
Break the old customs that fetter men fast!
Here is true victory, here is faith's crown—
One creed and one world, division thrown down!
Cast on the soil of your clay the heart's seed:
Promise of harvest to come is that seed!

Iqbal wrote this poem early in the twentieth century. The Panjab (or Punjab) peasant was indeed "trampled in dust" at that time. The Punjab is the heart of Pakistan today, but in and around 1900, it was a provincial backwater, valued by the British conquerors only for its wheat and its proximity to the mountain passes that led to neighboring Afghanistan. The British, and perhaps many of the Punjabis themselves, had forgotten that a long, tumultuous, and glorious history lay in the dust of the Punjab: Alexander the Great walked there, the teachings of Buddha and Kabir had been preached there, and Islam had been carried there by Turkish warriors a thousand years earlier. Much of this was forgotten. Iqbal spoke truly when he wrote, "Deep in that dust has been smothered your flame."

Punjab under the British Empire

Iqbal felt passionate about the Punjab. He was born there, at Sialkot, in 1877. First educated in Lahore, he went to England and studied both at Cambridge and at a German university

Taming the mighty Indus River to make Pakistan's agriculture more productive was one of the great successes of British colonial rule. Irrigation projects like this one first began around 1850.

between 1905 and 1908. He received his doctorate and was even knighted by the British government in 1922, but his deepest allegiance was to the Punjab.

Iqbal referred to the Punjab as it was: the breadbasket of British-ruled India. The British had begun a series of canals and irrigation projects around 1850, and the result was that the Punjab, already known for the quality of its crops, now began to produce those crops in much larger amounts. Punjabi irrigation was seen as one of the glories of the British Empire, a testament to the beneficent influence of the British rule, but Iqbal saw it differently. "Not in that darkness is Life's river fed!"

During his years in England and Germany, Iqbal had become well acquainted with the major philosophers of the day. He first learned, and then rejected the major teachings of the European philosophers. Iqbal came to believe that Europe and the West were in a state of moral and intellectual decline. Rejuvenation would not come from European cities, argued Iqbal. It would come from a resurgence of Eastern peoples, informed both by their magnificent histories and by the Muslim faith. In 1930, he became president of the Muslim League, a religious and political organization devoted to finding a new way of life for the Muslim peoples of the subcontinent.

Iqbal believed that the Eastern peoples—those of the Indian subcontinent in particular—were held back by customs that had developed over the past 3,000 years: those of tribe and of caste.

Tradition and Caste

Caste is a Portuguese word that came to India in the sixteenth century, but it refers to a social ranking that has governed life on the subcontinent for millennia. The caste system differentiated and discriminated among the people of India. A person was born into a certain caste, and remained there. There was no concept of self-improvement leading to social advancement. One was what one was born to be.

A tribe is the farthest extension of family loyalty. Tribal customs and loyalty shape people's minds and hearts more deeply than nationality.

Tribal loyalties were especially strong in British India, and Iqbal saw these as part of the formula that kept the Indian peoples from attaining the glory they deserved. Pakistanis today remain a strongly tribal people, and the Pashtuns—who live on the border between Pakistan and Afghanistan—are the largest autonomous tribal group on Earth.

Iqbal spelled out his answer to these dilemmas of tribe and caste in his poetry:

> Here is true victory, here is faith's crown—
> One creed and one world, division thrown down!
> Cast on the soil of your clay the heart's seed:
> Promise of harvest to come is that seed!

"One creed and one world" meant that Islam would be triumphant. Iqbal was not a militaristic or vainglorious man, but he clearly believed that the Muslim faith was the best the world had to offer, and that it should spread everywhere. When he referred to "division thrown down!" Iqbal probably meant British India, in which millions of people divided by tribe and caste were easily ruled by a small number of English soldiers and administrators.

Land of the Pure

During the 1930s, a group of Indian students at Cambridge University in England designed an acronym for the country that Iqbal envisioned. They put together eight letters: P-A-K-I-S-T-A-N. In Urdu, the language of the educated classes, the word means "Land of the Pure," but it also stands for some of the land and landscape of the country. The "P" stands for Punjab; the "A" stands for Afghan; the "K" stands for Kashmir (which is now divided between Pakistan and India); and the "STAN" is for Baluchistan. This acronym, made around 1933, has become the name of the country that was carved out of Iqbal's

Pakistan is a part of the Indian subcontinent, which also includes India, Bangladesh, Nepal, and Bhutan. India and Pakistan became separate nations in August 1947 when the British withdrew from the region.

vision and the political compromises that followed the British departure from the subcontinent in 1947.

Iqbal died in 1938, just nine years before the Indian subcontinent was released from British rule. Two nations rather than one emerged: India and Pakistan. Iqbal's beliefs helped create the nation of Pakistan, the "Land of the Pure."

The Indus River has long been the lifeline of Pakistan and the center of its trade and culture. Even in the late twentieth century, the river remained a vital part of the Pakistani economy.

CHAPTER

2

From the Mouth of the Lion to the Sea of Sinbad: The Land and Waters of Pakistan

Of all these names the first seems to me the most apt, for the Indus is a lion throughout its course. It is beautiful, powerful, unpredictable and dangerous. . . . both in time and space, the Indus is cruel, and as ruthless and cunning as any lion.

—Jean Fairely, *The Lion River: The Indus*

A mighty river stretches about 1,900 miles (3,058 kilometers) from headwaters to mouth, and passes through terrain that is difficult and sometimes terrifying to the people who dare to venture there.

How many people, great and small, have crossed that river, floated on it, or planted their crops next to it? How many untold millions of people depended upon the river during the centuries of recorded and unrecorded history? One can get a sense of the answer through a list of the military and spiritual leaders who either passed over the Indus River, or spent their lives along its banks: the Buddha, Mahavira, Guru Nanak, Alexander the Great, Chandragupta, his grandson Ashoka, Babur and his grandson Akbar; other Muslim and Moghul lords; Sikh military men; British subjects of Queen Victoria. The list goes on and on. Even though it is less known to Westerners than the Nile or the Amazon, the Indus has probably seen more "celebrities" than either of the other rivers.

Rivers are one of the key ingredients of civilization. Humans need water even more than they need food. Many wars have started—and may start in the future—over competition for water rights, including rights to the Indus and its precious water.

Rivers are also an important means of identifying people and places. When one discusses Paris, for example, one uses the terms "right bank" and "left bank" of the Seine River. The "right" and "left" are used as if one is looking downstream toward the coast. Therefore, in Paris, the "right" bank is to the north, and the "left" bank is to the south of the Seine. We will use these same directions in regard to the Indus River—the central spine of the land of Pakistan.

Because of the emphasis on Western geography in the United States, the very name of the Indus is less familiar than the Nile, Tigris, Euphrates, or Tiber. Even so, the Indus is as great as any of these rivers; it ranks among the most important

Much of the eastern half of Pakistan is flat alluvial lowland that is less than 600 feet (180 meters) in elevation, drained by the Indus River and its tributaries. The western half of the country is a region of rugged plateaus, hills, mountains, and narrow valleys.

in the world in terms of length and the power of its flow. The Indus has given life to civilization in Pakistan for more than 4,000 years, and gave the entire Indian subcontinent its name. For all these reasons, it is vital to know the Indus in order to come to know Pakistan.

The Indus

The Indus has had many names given to it by fishermen, tradesmen, villagers, and peasants throughout the centuries, or even millennia. One of the most apt names was given by the Tibetan people who live near the river's source: Father Indus, the Lion River.

No Westerner saw the upper reaches of the Indus until hardy Portuguese priests went there in the seventeenth century. The priests wrote a report that made the countryside sound dismal and depressing—perhaps because they wanted to discourage other Europeans from going there. As a result, it took until about 1907 for the first European—Sven Hedin—to find the source of the Indus.

Hedin, who was Swedish, first traveled north to Lake Manasarowar in Tibet. The local peoples told him that this lake was the source for four great rivers: the Brahmaputra, Indus, Ganges, and Sutlej. Hedin felt confident the lake was not the source of the Indus, but he began his explorations there anyway. Moving around in an inflatable boat he had brought with him, Hedin confirmed that the lake was not the source of the rivers, then continued to explore northward. He went first to Mount Kalias, 22,000 feet (6,706 meters) high, and the center of many Tibetan traditions. About 30 miles (48 kilometers) north of Mount Kalias and 80 miles north of Lake Manasarowar, he found "an insignificant stream," and then a "tiny brook" at about 17,000 feet (5,182 meters) above sea level in the glaciated hillsides. Hedin, who had a sense of the dramatic, wrote, "Here I stood and saw the Indus emerge from the lap of the earth."

The natives call the spot Hedin described *Singi Kabab*, which means "the Mouth of the Lion."

Some people still debate whether Hedin found the exact spot. There are hundreds, if not thousands, of springs and brooks that feed into the Indus. It is possible another one may be found someday that is older, longer, and more central to the river than Hedin's. In any event, Hedin estimated the source for the Indus, which gives life to the dry and dusty lands of Pakistan. It is difficult for Westerners to reach the source today, because it lies within Tibet, which is controlled by the People's Republic of China.

By accepting Hedin's source, the description of the Indus can be narrowed down to say: it rises in Tibet; it runs through mountain gorges with the Himalayas to its south and the Karakorum range to its north; it descends from 17,000 to 5,000 feet (5,182 to 1,524 meters) above sea level as it crosses the top of India; it then makes a sharp left turn, and heads to the plains of Pakistan; from there, it finds its way to the Arabian Sea.

Rising in western Tibet, the Indus runs on a course due west for some time. In its first 500 miles (805 kilometers), the river drops 12,000 feet (3,658 meters)—from 17,000 feet (5,182 meters) above sea level to about 5,000 (1,524 meters). As the gap between the Himalayas to the south and the Karakorum to the north narrows, the Indus becomes a churning, angry river, seeking to break through the rock that confines it. It winds its way through the provinces of Ladakh and Baltistan, and then makes a sharp but short turn to the south.

As the Indus resumes its westward course, on its left (southern) bank one can see Nanga Parbat, 26,000 feet (7,925 meters) high and one of the most impressive mountains in the world. This was the mountain that the German climber Heinrich Harrer wanted to climb in 1939. He set off for it, but was detained by the British at the beginning of

World War II. Harrer escaped captivity, and went over the Himalayas into Tibet, where he spent time with the child Dalai Lama. Harrer's account, *Seven Years in Tibet*, is a masterpiece of adventure literature, and was made into a film in 1997.

Harrer did not conquer Nanga Parbat; no one did until 1953, the same year that Edmund Hillary and Tensing Norgay climbed Mount Everest. The forbidding mountain still looms over the Indus River.

About 75 miles (121 kilometers) past Nanga Parbat, the Indus turns south again. There is no alternative. The Hindu Kush mountains lie directly ahead, and there is no choice but to turn south and enter the alluvial plains that make up the bulk of Pakistan.

The Indus River emerges from the mountains onto the Potwar Plateau, which ranges between 1,000 and 2,000 feet (305 to 610 meters) above sea level. Almost at once, the Indus encounters a new obstacle—a great dam at Tarbela. Built between 1965 and 1980, the dam stands 469 feet (143 meters) high and is 2,264 feet (690 meters) thick at the base. Along with the Mangla Dam on the Chenab River, the Tarbela Dam makes irrigation possible for the entire region of the Punjab, which lies just below it.

The Northwest Frontier Province and the Khyber Pass

The Northwest Frontier Province (NWFP) lies on the right bank as the Indus descends from the mountains to the plains. As a traveler leaves the Indus and heads west, he moves steadily uphill to the NWFP, also known as the land of the Pathans (or Pashtuns).

This is a landscape as rich in imagery as it has been in historic confrontations between peoples who wanted to secure the mountain passes. The Northwest Frontier Province is the traditional gateway between Afghanistan and Pakistan, and the point of entry to the entire Indian subcontinent.

These village women, living in the desert in eastern Pakistan, searched for water during a deadly drought in May 2000.

This is the land in which the "Great Game" was played between British and Russian scouts in the nineteenth century. Both British and Russian adventurers wanted to secure this area for their nations.

The Great Game began in the 1840s when the British entered what is now Pakistan. They defeated the Sikhs in a short and bloody war and proceeded to make central Pakistan a British province. The Northwest Frontier Province was the gateway from that land to Afghanistan, and therefore was like a swinging door: it opened from either end.

The Russians, who had expanded steadily into central Asia since about 1800, were eager to find a way into the Indian subcontinent. The only natural and logical way for them to do so was through the Khyber Pass, which is full of romance, legends, and smugglers even today.

About 40 miles long, the Khyber Pass runs from Peshawar in Pakistan to Kabul in Afghanistan. It is a natural gateway located more than 10,000 feet (3,048 meters) above sea level. Here, Alexander the Great and Babur the Moghul entered the subcontinent. Nineteenth-century Russians intended to emulate these predecessors.

The Russians were thwarted by British scouts and agents who played the Great Game between about 1850 and 1895. In 1897, British Lord Durand undertook a major scouting and surveying expedition. Its result was the Durand Line, drawn between British India and Russian-dominated Afghanistan. The line is still the official border today. It separates the Pathans (Pashtuns), half of whom are in Afghanistan and half of whom are in Pakistan. This division has led to calls for a new country to be created called Pashtunistan.

A recent description of the Khyber Pass was made by Stephen Alter, an Indian of American descent:

In essence a road provides access to trade and territory while a border restricts movement along that route. The intersection of these two lines on a map represents specific points of conflict. Nowhere in the world is this more evident than along the mountainous frontier of Pakistan and Afghanistan. The history of South Asia has long been dictated by the accessibility of routes across the Hindu Kush and the generally unsuccessful lines of defence that were put up to block invaders and regulate trade.

The Khyber Pass is frequented today by smugglers carrying goods on bicycles. They race up and down the dangerous road to bring goods from one country to another. To them, the land is all the same; most of them belong to the tribe of Pashtuns who have long held the keys to this mountain terrain. For a true foreigner, the boundaries are obvious. As Stephen Alter wrote:

> Two kilometers beyond Landi Kotal we came to a place called Michni Kandao. Here there was a signboard that read, "Foreigners are not permitted beyond this point." Though the mountains were obscured by a haze of dust, I could see just across into Afghanistan. The entire landscape was a khaki brown, except for the brightly painted buses, with bulging sides, that carried passengers to Torkham.

The Punjab

Leaving the Northwest Frontier Province, and returning to the Indus River allows a look at the Punjab (Land of Five Rivers), which stands on the river's left (eastern) bank.

The Punjab is made by the movement and eventual meeting of five rivers. Moving from east to west (from right to left on a map) they are the Jhelum, Chenab, Ravi, Beas, and Sutlej. The rivers join in the lower Punjab and form the last stretch of the mighty Indus River. One of the few solid agreements made between Pakistan and India concerns these rivers. Under the Waters Treaty of 1960, it was agreed that India would have exclusive use of the waters of the three easternmost rivers, and that Pakistan would have exclusive use of the Jhelum and Indus. So far this agreement has worked well for both nations.

Despite the great flow of waters, much of the area between the rivers was dry and arid until the British began irrigation projects around 1850. Since then, the Punjab has become the breadbasket for most of Pakistan. Cotton, jute, rice, millet, and other crops are produced there in great quantities.

The Grand Trunk Road slices neatly through the Punjab, beginning at Lahore, and making its way to Peshawar. This bisection from east to west parallels the more profound bisection that occurred when Pakistan and India were created. The Punjab was split between the two nations. Pakistan received about 63 percent of the land and a greater percentage of its people. Millions of people were affected by the event, and bitterness still exists on both sides of the border.

The dislocations caused by the separation are painful and have had long-lasting consequences. Because of the distrust and suspicion between India and Pakistan, a simple border crossing from Lahore in Pakistan to Amritsar in India can take about 15 hours. Stephen Alter chronicled his crossing in 1997:

> The temperature had been climbing since morning and it was now past noon, the air thick with humidity and flies. I found a place to sit down, next to the fence, which gave me a view of the custom's inspectors on the other side. For the next three hours I watched the lines move slowly forward as the officials put each traveler through an inquisition. There was something vindictive in the way they treated the passengers, as if these were traitors or enemies of the state simply because they were crossing the border.

Whether they live in Pakistan or in India, many people of the Punjab area simply call themselves "Punjabis," which was their geographic name long before the two nations were created in 1947. Although anxiety and tension exist at nearly every place along the border between Pakistan and India, the sadness that accompanies the suspicion is most evident in the Punjab, where the natural landscape was cut in half in an attempt to find a solution to religious tensions.

Punjab ("Land of Five Rivers") may sound like a well-watered, harmonious place, but without irrigation, half of it would be a desert. The heat is intense—a mixture of dust and humidity that can overwhelm even the strongest workers. Dams are a vital necessity to the well-being of the Punjab, which is the political and cultural center of Pakistan.

Many forces are at work throughout the landscape. Pakistan is rarely harmonious—or bland. Instead, it is a land—and a nation—of remarkable contrasts.

Baluchistan

As one travels farther south along the Indus, the landscape divides into the province of Baluchistan on the west bank and the province of Sind on the east bank.

Baluchistan is the least populous part of the country. It contains about 40 percent of the nation's land, but only about 4 percent of the people live there. It is a hard, dusty landscape that few foreigners have seen. Alexander the Great and his army nearly perished in 323 B.C. when they left the Indus and headed here on their way to Persia. Of the many images of Alexander the Great, one of the most popular shows the Macedonian conqueror receiving a helmet of water collected by his followers. Urged to drink the water to keep his strength, Alexander poured the precious liquid out in the desert to show he would share the hardships with his men. Alexander and his men did reach Persia, but few conquerors since have chosen the same route.

Baluchistan remains the most undeveloped part of Pakistan. Tribal peoples weave cloth the same way they did 1,000 years ago, and make a meager living by moving their herds from south to north during the summer months. Still, Baluchistan often inspires admiration among the people who see it. Historian Arnold J. Toynbee wrote: "Have you ever doubted Man's heroism? If you have, plunge southward from Quetta into Central Baluchistan, and your doubts will have been dispelled long before you have reached Khuzdar."

This is some of the most desolate landscape on the face of the earth. Few rivers flow through Baluchistan. Camels and packhorses find occasional oases, but there is very little true relief from the parched conditions. This is not a dramatic desert of sand, like those found in Saudi Arabia, but a hard, dry land surface that receives only about five inches of rainfall per year. Sand columns abound, and travelers have often commented that Baluchistan closely resembled the moon.

This is where the Indus flows into the Arabian Sea. Along its journey of 1,900 miles (3,058 kilometers) from the mountains of Tibet, the Indus generates three times as much flow as the Nile, and ten times as much as the Colorado River in the American Southwest. Today, the mighty Indus displays less of its former magnificence because of the large number of dams upstream and the diversion of water for irrigation.

Even with its reduced current and flow, the Indus still has about four branches that empty into the Arabian Sea, creating a delta that rivals the Lena Delta in Siberia and the Mississippi Delta south of New Orleans. Like those other deltas, the Indus River Delta has branches that change their course periodically; that is why the once great town of Bambhore is small today, while Karachi has grown to be a huge metropolis.

Located just west of the Indus Delta, Karachi is an enormous port city. Just 150 years ago it was a small town, and even by 1947, it had only 400,000 inhabitants. Today, it has between 12 million and 14 million people, and is one of the most troubled places on the subcontinent. The gap between rich and poor is especially evident in Karachi. Upper-class businessmen live in homes that resemble forts, while hundreds of thousands of unemployed people roam the streets, occasionally holding large demonstrations. It is perhaps fortunate for government officials that the Pakistani capital was moved north to Islamabad in 1962. Unfortunately,

Karachi has become an enormous city that rivals many Western cities in both size and importance. Unfortunately, Karachi is also plagued by many problems, including a severe gap between the rich and poor that often leads to violence.

the move gave an impression of abandonment, as if Karachi's problems are too great to be solved.

As a port city, Karachi is as important to Pakistan as New York City, San Francisco, and New Orleans combined are to the United States. Karachi's influence reaches far upstream; it is the major port for Afghanistan, too. However, Karachi is not a popular tourist destination. Foreigners use its excellent airport and then quickly depart for other parts of the nation.

East and north of Karachi are the ruins of Mohenjo-daro, the site of one of the oldest civilizations in human history. Tourists can see the mud-dried bricks that supported a city of perhaps 50,000 people between 2500 and 1700 B.C. It is not known exactly what happened to Mohenjo-daro. For generations, it was believed that this early civilization was wiped out by Indo-Aryans who migrated from the north. It is just as possible, however, that Mohenjo-daro fell victim to the shifting waters of the Indus.

Sind

East of Mohenjo-daro, and east of the Indus River, lies the province of Sind. It is an arid landscape that has been partially transformed by a major dam upstream at Sukhor. Even so, Sind is one of the least hospitable areas of Pakistan to foreigners, and it is the place where tribal and village lords hold the most power. Though there are democratic elections throughout Pakistan, it is well known that villagers cannot vote against the wishes of their landlords in the Sind.

The Indus River Delta is one of the world's largest. Occupying an area of 3,000 square miles (4,828 square kilometers), it is as flat as a pancake. In the delta, there are small fishing boats. People search for crabs, but this is one of the most remote ends to a great river seen anywhere. It resembles the Mississippi River below New Orleans.

The Indus moves about one million tons of silt a day, and that silt has been piling up in the delta for thousands of years. The coast today is between 50 and 80 miles (80 and 129 km) farther south than it was 2,000 years ago, and the silt keeps piling up.

Finally, the Indus, in more than half a dozen shallow channels, meets the Arabian Sea. For at least 20 miles

(32 kilometers) out, the grayish-green of the river mixes with the blue-green of the sea. It is a magical spot, but also a lonely one. Like the tiny spring where it begins, the ending of the Indus is remote to humans. At least half of the great Lion River remains a mystery, even to those who have spent a lifetime beside it.

Beyond the silt and the breakers lies the Arabian Sea, which was once known as the Sea of Sinbad. Perhaps it is fitting that the Indus begins in a place of mystery, near Mount Kalias, and ends on a lonely coastal spot that summons up images from a bygone age.

During Pakistan's long history, its people developed one of the world's oldest and most sophisticated civilizations. Today, the legacy of this culture can be found in landmarks such as the ruins of Mohenjo-Daro.

CHAPTER

3

Pakistan Through Time

Few countries have weathered as many changes in government, religion, and society as Pakistan has. From the days of the Indus Valley civilization to the modern-day Islamic Republic of Pakistan, the land and its peoples have undergone change time and again. A short list of governments and dynasties follows:

Indus Civilization:	2500–1700 B.C.
Vedic Period:	1700–600 B.C.
States:	300 B.C.–A.D. 300
Fragmentation:	A.D. 300–1000
Delhi Sultanate:	1250–1526
Moghul Dynasty:	1526–1760
Warring States:	1760–1860
British Raj:	1860–1947
Republic of Pakistan:	1947–

To this list must be added a second to show the appearance and development of different religions in Pakistan.

Tribal, Pantheistic:	Prehistoric
Polytheistic, formal:	2500–1700 B.C.
Vedic, Aryan:	1600 B.C.
Buddhist and Jain:	600 B.C.
Christianity:	First century A.D.
Muslim:	Eighth century A.D.
Sikh:	Fifteenth century A.D.
Kabir:	Fifteenth century A.D.

Future archaeological digs may prove current theories wrong, but most experts believe civilization began in Pakistan around 2500 B.C. Pakistan was one of the three early "cradles of civilization." The other two were in Egypt, centered on the Nile River, and in Mesopotamia, centered between the Tigris and Euphrates rivers. For centuries, students of history considered these two the major cradles of civilization until a series of archaeological digs done in the 1920s indicated that there was a third cradle along the banks of the Indus River in what is now Pakistan.

Indus Valley Civilization

Sometime around 2500 B.C., a civilization arose that had its center in about half a dozen cities that were sprinkled from the Punjab to the middle of the Sind. All these cities had populations of around 25,000 to 30,000, but the best preserved sites and the ones that have yielded the most to archaeologists, are Mohenjo-Daro in the Sind, and Harappa in the Punjab. Even though more finds have been made in Mohenjo-Daro, scholars tend to call this early civilization either "Harappan" or "Indus Valley civilization."

The Harappans, as the entire civilization was called, employed advanced building and irrigation techniques.

Mud-dried bricks (*adobe* in Spanish) were put together to make houses, apartments, and towns, and canals were dug to make the most use of the waters of the Indus River. Some scholars suggest that the Harappans achieved a level of comfort, for the upper class at least, that exceeded the living standards of many people in India and Pakistan today.

The Harappans used a written script, but it has never been deciphered. It bears no resemblance to the languages used in Egypt or Mesopotamia. About all that scholars have been able to use are the seals that are in pictographic form. They usually show animals and trade goods. This meager evidence suggests that the Harappans were a merchant-oriented people, and they may have been the eastern extension of a trade network that reached at least as far as Mesopotamia. Until the Harappan script is deciphered, a certain amount of guesswork is required to discuss the Harappans and the Indus Valley civilization.

The Indus civilization declined after about 2000 B.C. and virtually disappeared after about 1700 B.C. How and why this happened has been the subject of scholarly debates for at least 50 years. There are two scenarios that are considered most likely, although the reason may in fact be a combination of the two, or some other theory that may soon arise.

First is the Aryan invasion theory. There is no doubt that there were a group of tribal peoples collectively called "Aryan," and that they entered what is now Pakistan between about 2000 and 1500 B.C. The Aryans came from the steppes of central Asia, and they entered Pakistan with new animals—sheep, horses, cattle—and new weapons made of bronze, which allowed them to first invade, and then dominate the local peoples. Whether the Aryans actually conquered the cities of the Indus River valley, or whether those cities suffered from a long, slow decline is uncertain. What is certain is that the cities were practically extinct by about 1700 B.C.

The second theory is that the Indus River changed its course enough times, and to such a significant degree, that the cities of the Harappan civilization fell when they lost their water supplies.

The next 1,000 years belong to a period known as "Vedic," or "Brahmanic." The Vedic and Brahmanic texts come from an oral tradition that developed between about 1500 and 500 B.C., and much of the Hindu religion comes from these early beginnings. The scene and site of civilization shifted away from Pakistan during this period and concentrated on the Gangetic Plain—the lands around the Ganges River in central and eastern India. Pakistan was an isolated place during this period, but it remained—and always will remain—important because of its position at the western door to the Indian subcontinent.

During the Vedic era, the divisions between ranks of the society of peoples of the subcontinent became firmer. Although the word *caste* did not come until later, Indians (people of the subcontinent) began to be divided between Brahmans (priests), Kshatriyas (warriors), Vaishyas (merchants), and Sudras (serfs). It is likely that the lighter-skinned Aryans occupied the top two castes and that the darker-skinned original inhabitants made up the two lower castes. The specific rules and regulations of each caste group became more defined. Nothing was more insulting to an Indian than to suggest that he or she perform work that was not appropriate to his or her caste. Pakistan today is a caste-free society, although the Republic of India has retained many of the social ranks.

Buddhism and Jainism

Perhaps in response to Brahmanic culture and the development of the caste system, two major new religions were founded in India during the sixth century B.C. Buddhism developed through the life and teachings of Siddhartha Gautama, later known as the Buddha. Born into a warrior caste in northern India, Siddhartha enjoyed a life of pleasure and ease until the age of 29. At that time, he voluntarily renounced his position to spend years searching for enlightenment, or "spiritual truth." After many years of apparently unsuccessful searching, Siddartha attained enlightenment as he sat under a tree. He came to the decision, or realization, that all of life is suffering, and that the only cure for life's suffering is nonattachment: to avoid becoming attached to any person, place, or thing. Desire, in other words, is the cause of all suffering.

Known to his followers as the Buddha, the Enlightened One, Siddartha traveled and taught for the rest of his life. His teachings are encompassed in the Eight-Fold Path, which includes concepts such as right thought, right action, right livelihood, and right speech. The Buddha's teachings took root in what is now India, and spread to Pakistan, Tibet, Burma, and eventually, to China. Everywhere the Buddhist faith travels, it brings with it the dual message of compassion and non-attachment.

Mahavira may have been a contemporary of the Buddha. Mahavira believed in many of the principles taught by the Buddha, but went further in relation to the concept of nonviolence. Mahavira expanded nonviolence to mean noninjury to every living thing, including flies, worms, and insects. Many scholars have pointed out the negative implications of Mahavira's beliefs: If worms and insects cannot be harmed, then how can one fish, farm, or plow the soil?

Perhaps because of these difficulties, Mahavira's faith did not become as popular or as widespread as that of the Buddha. Still, the religion he founded—Jainism—remains important. There are more than 2 million Jainists in India and Pakistan today.

Alexander the Great Arrives

About 250 years after the founding of these two new faiths, Alexander the Great appeared on the middle reaches of the Indus River. It is often said that 326 B.C.—the year of his appearance—is the first definite date in the history of the Indian subcontinent. Alexander crossed the Indus and fought a battle against King Porus of the Punjab. Porus had elephants, the first Alexander's troops had seen. The battle was fierce, but Alexander prevailed, as he usually did. He and Porus then became friends and firm allies.

Confident in his destiny, Alexander wanted to push on into India. His Macedonian soldiers, however, weary of a decade of military campaigns, staged a sit-down protest against their leader. They refused to go any farther. They wanted to return to their wives and families in Macedonia.

Although he was furious over his men's disobedience, Alexander agreed to return home. He built a fleet of boats, and the Macedonian army floated down the length of the Indus River. Alexander divided his army into two sections. The first (and luckier) men boarded the boats and sailed along the Arabian coast on their way back to Persia. The second group went overland with Alexander, through the deserts of lower Baluchistan.

The Gedrosian Desert, through which Alexander and his men marched, is one of the most inhospitable places on Earth. Many men died from the conditions. Alexander and the hardiest soldiers survived. They came out of the desert and reached Babylon, Mesopotamia, where Alexander died at the age of 31 or 32. During his short, whirlwind life, Alexander had impacted the lives of peoples from the Straits of Dardanelles in what is now Turkey to the banks of the Indus River.

ALEXANDER M.

P.B.F

Before he reached age 30, Alexander the Great of Macedonia had conquered large sections of the known world. Alexander and his troops fought a fierce battle against King Porus of the Punjab during their travels. Then they faced an even more dangerous experience as they crossed the harsh desert landscape of what is now Pakistan's Baluchistan region.

The Mauryan Kingdom

Pakistani tradition says that in his brief six months on the banks of the Indus, Alexander met an ambitious young Indian prince named Chandragupta. This man saw Alexander's power and grandeur and decided to emulate him.

Within 30 years of Alexander's departure, Chandragupta had built the foundations of the first truly indigenous kingdom of the Indian subcontinent. Centered in what is now northwest India and Pakistan, the new Mauryan kingdom extended for nearly 1,000 miles (1,609 kilometers) in an east-west line.

Chandragupta's grandson, Ashoka (also spelled *Asoka*) became the most renowned of the Mauryan kings. More is known about Ashoka than any previous Indian leader because of the edicts his officials carved in stones. These edicts tell a story of an ambitious, warlike king, who converted to Buddhism and then came close to becoming a true "philosopher-king."

Ashoka made war on his neighbors, the Kringalis, in his youth, and was appalled by the death and destruction he caused. Changing his mind and his life, he became a Buddhist, and had edicts carved. Reminders of the sanctity of life, Ashoka's edicts are among the best-known depictions of a personal religious conversion from ancient history.

The Mauryan dynasty weakened after Ashoka, and it was in ruins by the time of Jesus Christ's birth. In the centuries that followed, Pakistan and northern India were overrun by countless invasions from the north, over the Khyber Pass route. In Western history they are known as the Scythians (horse people of the plains of southern Russia), but on the subcontinent they are known as the Sakas, who established a kingdom that lasted for nearly 200 years. They were followed by the Kushans and others.

In the sixth century A.D., a Chinese monk came to Pakistan and India, looking for relics of the Buddha. Known as Hsunag-Tsuang, this remarkable man made it from China to India over the Himalayas, and, after a stay of nearly 20 years, he returned the same way, taking with him hundreds of Buddhist books and relics. Chinese Buddhism is a direct descendant of this one man's efforts.

Islam

Yet another religion, however, was about to appear. It made itself known in the seventh century A.D., and found its way to the subcontinent in the eighth century. This was Islam, or the Muslim faith (Muslim means "one who submits to the will of Allah [the Muslim name for God]").

Founded by the Prophet Muhammad around 620 A.D., the new faith spread rapidly from its birthplace on the Arabian Peninsula. Fortified by this strict new monotheistic faith, the Arabs conquered Persia, took most of North Africa, and entered Spain in A.D. 711.

At about the same time, Arab Muslims first arrived in Pakistan. Unlike most invaders, they came by sea, landing near the mouths of the Indus River. Within one generation, the Arabs had become masters of the Sind. This group of conquerors did not expand farther. They remained in the Sind, giving that area a different character from the rest of Pakistan for some time.

Full-scale Muslim invasions came later, through the Khyber Pass. Muhammad of Ghazni, known to many Muslim scholars as a Defender of the Faith and to many outsiders as a bandit and plunderer, made no less than 17 invasions of Pakistan and northern India. Muhammad did not succeed in his goal of creating a Muslim Pakistan, but many of the tribal peoples in the northwest were converted to Islam during the eleventh and twelfth centuries.

The Delhi Sultanate

A true Muslim state was first set up around 1325 when the Delhi Sultanate was established. The sultans who ruled a swath of northern India and Pakistan did so loosely, giving much authority to regional rulers. It was a Muslim state, but it was not a theocracy. The period of the Delhi Sultanate (1325–1526) was marked by better relations between Hindus and Muslims than would later be the case.

In the last few decades of the Delhi Sultanate, two new holy men arose to suggest new ways of understanding. Guru Nanak and Kabir were contemporaries.

Born in the city of Benares, Guru Nanak led a normal life until his thirties, when he experienced an awakening. Its basic message was quite simple: "There is no Hindu, there is no Mussalman [Muslim]" in the eyes of God. If ever there was a messenger and a message who had a hope to unite India's religions, it was Guru Nanak.

Born in northern India about the same time as Guru Nanak, Kabir was a free spirit who avoided nearly all formal religion. When asked what faith he followed, Kabir replied, "No book, no creed." Kabir disliked the caste system, formalized Hinduism, and the conflicts between Hindus and Muslims in India.

Kabir is remembered today as a great saint, revered by Hindus and Muslims alike. Guru Nanak is known as the founder of the new faith of the Sikhs. Blending aspects of both Hinduism and Islam, the Sikhs came to dominate the land of the Punjab.

Guru Nanak was a peaceful man, but in the mid-seventeenth century, the Sikhs became known as warriors. They were hired as bodyguards, treasure keepers, and mercenaries. By the time the British came to India and Pakistan in the nineteenth century, the Sikhs were considered the best fighters on the subcontinent.

The Mughal Empire

All previous invasions or incursions had come either through the northwestern passes or by a short sea trip from Persia. In the early fifteenth century, two new invasions came, including one by a very long route, completely around Africa.

Two invasions came at almost exactly the same moment, in the early sixteenth century. In 1526, Babur, who was a Turco-Mongol, invaded Pakistan through the Khyber Pass. He

The love of art and culture that flourished during the Mughal Empire can still be seen in some of Pakistan's current landmarks, such as this college in Lahore, which boasts elaborate brickwork.

defeated the armies of the Delhi Sultanate and by the time of his death in 1530, he had set the early foundation of what would become the Mughal Empire (1526–1760). *Mughal* is a corruption of the word *Mongol*. Babur was a descendant of both Genghis Khan and Tamerlane, the great Mongol leaders. Just the same, Babur brought a tradition of interest in art, poetry, and flowers that gave his Mughal dynasty a very different public image from that of the early Mongols. This interest in art and culture continued through Babur's descendants. His great-grandson Shah Jehan built the Taj Mahal.

In about the same year that Babur arrived from the northwest, Portuguese sailors and missionaries arrived in the southern parts of the subcontinent. The Portuguese came to India on their search for the spices of the East. They built forts along the southern coast of India to resupply their ships as their sailors went all the way to the Spice Islands of Indonesia.

The Mughal descendants of Babur ruled the north region of India and Pakistan. They made their capital at Lahore, today the center of Pakistani cultural and intellectual life. Their summer capital, built to escape the tremendous heat of the Punjab, was located in Sringhar, Kashmir.

The British Raj

Meanwhile, the Portuguese continued to hold small sections of southern India. The Portuguese, however, were replaced by the Dutch in the seventeenth century, who were then supplanted by the British and the French in the eighteenth century.

In 1757, Englishman Robert Clive won an important battle at Plassey in eastern India. From that day on, it became clear that the British would dominate the southern part of the subcontinent. Clive was not followed by British officials right away. For the next 80 years, the British East India Company managed British interests in India as a private, commercial concern. Only after the "Great Mutiny" of 1857–1858, did the British government change its policy. Queen Victoria became Empress of India, and India (including Pakistan) became the "jewel in the crown" of the British Empire.

The British Raj (the word *raj* derives from "one who rules") was a mixture of benevolence and despotism. The British thoroughly controlled southern India, but left a number of northern sections in the hands of local rulers such as maharajas. Pakistan, the western frontier of British India, was treated with great importance. Not only was this area vulnerable to penetration by Russia, but the British also saw other things of great value in Pakistan, the people in particular.

After a short but bloody war, the British defeated the Sikhs and occupied the Punjab. The British went farther, into Afghanistan, but there, they received one of the rare defeats suffered by the armies of Queen Victoria. The First Afghan War (1838–1840) saw the virtual annihilation of a British force outside Kabul. From then on, the British sought to control the passes, rather than attempt to pacify the people of the mountains. The Pashtuns have never been truly subjugated by anyone.

Between about 1860 and 1920, the British brought significant improvements to India and Pakistan. Irrigation projects in the Punjab were begun through British initiative. The city of Karachi's value was recognized, and its population began to grow under British rule. Perhaps even more important, the Sikhs, Muslims, Hindus, Christians, Zoroastrians, and others of the subcontinent knew they had equal status under British law, as long as they were not accused of assaulting or robbing a *Sahib*, or white-skinned ruler.

The Partition of India

After about 1920, however, enthusiasm for the British government waned. The Muslim League, founded in 1910, began to develop the idea of an independent Muslim Republic in Pakistan. Meanwhile, Mohandas Gandhi and others carried out a program of nonviolent resistance to British rule.

The British officers and viceroy considered Gandhi just a nuisance at first. During the 1930s, though, as he conducted hunger strikes and continued to insist on nonviolent methods, the British began to see the power of this movement.

World War II drained the British treasury and the will of the British people to maintain their great overseas empire. By early 1947, negotiations were in full swing for a British withdrawal from the subcontinent.

Mohandas Gandhi, who struggled to win independence for India, became known as "Mahatma," a title often translated as "Great Soul." Gandhi's dream of a united India—in which Muslims and Hindus could live in peace—ultimately has not come true.

From the beginning, Gandhi had dreamed, written, and spoken of a united India—an India one and indivisible. In the months that preceded independence, Muhammad ali-Jinnah, leader of the Muslim League, began to demand that two—rather than one—nations be created after the British evacuated, one for Hindus and one for Muslims. Gandhi resisted bitterly, claiming that "The right eye of India is Hindu, and its left eye is Muslim." It was Jinnah's vision that prevailed, however, and at midnight on August 14, 1947, two nations were created from the region that had been the British Raj.

American readers who opened *The New York Times* found articles about the Indian subcontinent all through the opening page and sections:

INDIA AND PAKISTAN BECOME NATIONS;
CLASHES CONTINUE
Ceremonies at New Delhi and Karachi Mark
Independence for 400,000,000 Persons.

New Delhi, Friday, Aug. 15—India achieved her long-sought independence today through the transfer of British power to two dominions into which that land of 400,000,000 persons has been divided: India and Pakistan.

Ceremonies in New Delhi proclaimed the new nation of India. Ceremonies in Karachi commemorated the birth of the new nation of Pakistan. The Indian subcontinent, indeed the Asian world, would never be the same again.

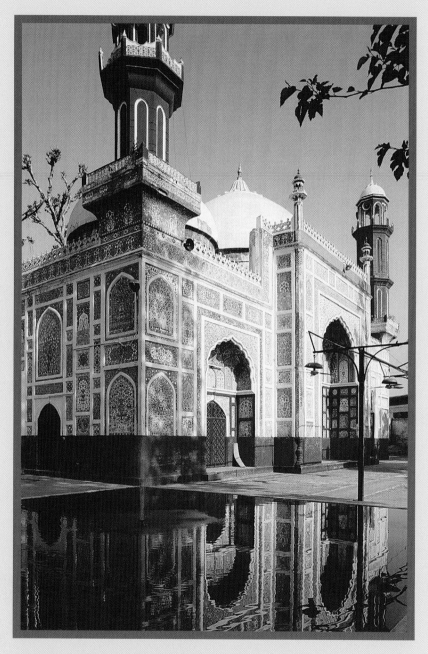

Most Pakistanis consider themselves first and foremost Muslims, rather than citizens of the nation. Islam is extremely important to the people, who worship at beautiful mosques like this one in Lahore.

4

The Peoples of Pakistan

What am I? Mussalman, Hindu, Jain, or Buddhist?
That is a hard knot.

—Rudyard Kipling, *Kim*

Since *Kim* was published in 1901, millions of readers around the world have thrilled to the story of the adolescent boy, the old lama (monk), and the middle-aged horse-trader. Written by Englishman Rudyard Kipling, *Kim* is a magnificent coming-of-age tale that combines remarkable story-telling with messages about the peoples and religions of British India. At one point in the book, the orphan boy Kim, who had an English father and an Indian mother, asks the horse-trader Mahbub Ali:

"What am I? Mussalman, Hindu, Jain, or Buddhist? That is a hard knot."

Mahbub Ali replied:

> Thou art beyond question an unbeliever, and therefore thou wilt be damned. So says my Law—or I think it does. But thou art also my Little Friend of all the World, and I love thee. So says my heart. This matter of creeds is like horseflesh. The wise man knows horses are good—that there is profit to be made from all; and for myself—but that I am a good Sunni and hate the men of Tirah—I could believe the same of all the Faiths. Now manifestly a Kathiawar mare taken from the sands of her birthplace and removed to the west of Bengal founders—nor is even a Balkh stallion (and there are no better horses than those of Balkh, were they not so heavy in the shoulder) of any account in the great Northern deserts beside the snow-camels I have seen. Therefore I say in my heart the Faiths are like the horses. Each has merit in its own country.

Though they were written in 1901, these words aptly describe the questions that continue to plague the people of Pakistan. Although 97 percent of them today are Muslim, they are descendants of Hindus, Persians, Jews, Zoroastrians, and others.

About 144 million people live in Pakistan. The nation's peoples are just as diverse as the landscape they inhabit. The Pakistanis display a great mixture of physical and cultural types, a mixture created by the numerous migrations and invasions that have occurred over the centuries. Roughly speaking, the major groups are: Punjabis, Sindhis, Pashtuns, Mohajirs, Baluchi, Brahuis, Kalashas, Burushos, Wahis, Baltis, Gujars, and refugees from Afghanistan. It is important to remember that this melting pot of peoples has existed for hundreds, if not thousands of years, even though the state of Pakistan is only slightly more than 50 years old.

Because the Punjabi people make up the majority of Pakistan's population, a great deal of Pakistani culture revolves around Punjabi ways. The people of Punjab hold on to many of their old traditions. These Punjabi women are making flat bread.

Punjabis

The Punjabis are the majority population of the nation. Based in the land of the Punjab, they are a distinct and recognizable group. Punjabis tend to be taller than many of their fellow Pakistanis, and they generally have lighter skins than most of the peoples to the south. It is likely that the Punjabis are of Aryan descent, but their point of origin is as mysterious to them as it is to outsiders. They share a long heritage of life in the Punjab, and a reputation as warriors. When the British first entered the Punjab in the 1840s, they designated the Punjabis a warrior people, and recruited many of them to serve in Queen Victoria's army.

The Punjabis have also endured a severe and painful split. The partition in 1947 left 63 percent of the Punjab in Pakistan's hands and the rest in India. Millions of people on both sides of the border feel the pain of the partition to this day. The bus ride from Amritsar, India, to Lahore, Pakistan, is the only point of entry that can connect long-separated families. Only in the Punjab, on both sides of the border, is there a strong sentiment for ending the partition and making the two countries one. In other parts of Pakistan, the idea of a reunion with India is considered impossible and undesirable.

A large majority of the administrators and leaders of the modern nation of Pakistan have been Punjabis. This numerical dominance is often resented by other Pakistani peoples, but the physical position of the Punjab—its centrality to the country—has made it almost an established fact that Punjabis will have the most influence in governmental affairs.

Sindhis

Sindhis live in the province of Sind, on the eastern side of the lower Indus River. Sindhis have long been seen as a people apart from the rest of Pakistan. This is because the desert areas of the Sind have isolated them from the north, and because this is where the Muslim faith first came to Pakistan in A.D. 711. Sindhis tend to see themselves as the "original" Muslims of Pakistan, and they view all the others as newcomers to the faith. Sindhis feel underrepresented at the high levels of government. They resent the fact that the Sind city of Karachi—which was once the capital of the nation—is often seen as a political backwater, and that nearly all decisions are made to the north in Islamabad. Within the great city of Karachi, many Sindhis resent the presence of the Mohajirs (refugees).

Physically, it is not easy to identify the Sindhis. They may be darker in complexion than the Punjabis, but enough cross-mixtures have occurred that the Sindhis tend to identify themselves culturally rather than ethnically.

One of the most extensive studies of the Sindhis was done in the mid-nineteenth century by British traveler and explorer Richard F. Burton. While studying the burial practices of the Sindhis, Burton commented:

> Every traveler in Sind must have remarked the immense tracts of graveyards which it contains. The reason of this disproportion between the cities of the dead and those of the living is, in the first place, that the people are fond of burying their kin in spots which are celebrated for sanctity, and secondly, they believe that by interring corpses close to the dust of their forefathers, the Ruham or souls of the departed, will meet and commune together after death. Hence it is that when a Sindhi dies in a foreign place, his heirs or friends will generally agree to remove the body to the family graveyard, at a certain period or within a stated time. The corpse is then exhumed, and carried in a box on horse or camel-back to its final destination. And it is believed that when such promise has been given, the two angels never visit the provisional tomb, but defer their questioning till the second interment takes place.

The Pashtuns

The easiest Pakistani cultural group to identify is the Pashtuns, who live in the Northwest Frontier Province and are cut off by the Afghan border from their relatives in Afghanistan. The Pashtuns are tall, slender, dark-haired, and highly excitable. They are very proud that they were never assimilated by the numerous conquerors who came through their area.

The Pashtuns, who are the world's largest autonomous tribal group, have a deep and powerful social code, which governs nearly all their actions. Known as *Pashtunwali* ("Way of the Pashtun"), the code is extremely male-centered. Pashtun men are expected to be cheerful, brave, and always hospitable. If a

Pashtun accepts a stranger into his home—however briefly—the Pashtun is expected to put all his own needs and desires into the background and to be completely at the service of his guest. This part of the code, called *Melmastia*, can extend to dangerous situations. If, for example, a guest is a criminal or a wanted person, the host is expected to lay down his own life if necessary to protect the guest. Very few exceptions are allowed to this rule.

Badal is the second part of the Pashtun code. *Badal* means "revenge," and Pashtun men are duty-bound to seek revenge for offenses, hostilities, and even for minor slights on their honor. Pashtuns are expected to wreak havoc either on the person who committed the offense, or on that person's family. There is no statute of limitations: Vengeance is often taken many years after the offense was committed. This part of the code has led to endless feuds and counter-feuds, which have caused the Pashtuns to lose the strength to resist outside forces.

Nanwatai is the third aspect of the code. It means "formal abasement." Because Pashtuns often fight each other, *Nanwatai* is meant to preserve the lives of the losers. The defeated are expected to show absolute submission to the victors, who are expected to be merciful and generous.

Nang, which means "honor," is the fourth part of the code. It refers to the duty of a Pashtun man to defend the honor of the women of his family or clan. Sometimes, *Nang* is taken to such an extreme that a Pashtun will seek retribution if an outsider takes a long look at a woman. This part of the code makes it very difficult for outsiders to infiltrate Pashtun clans.

Relations between the federal government in Islamabad and the Pashtuns are tricky at best. Pakistan recognizes the Pashtuns as an autonomous tribal group, and they do not pay taxes or vote in elections. Even so, they are recognized as one of the most important ethnic groups within Pakistan—and certainly the most dangerous.

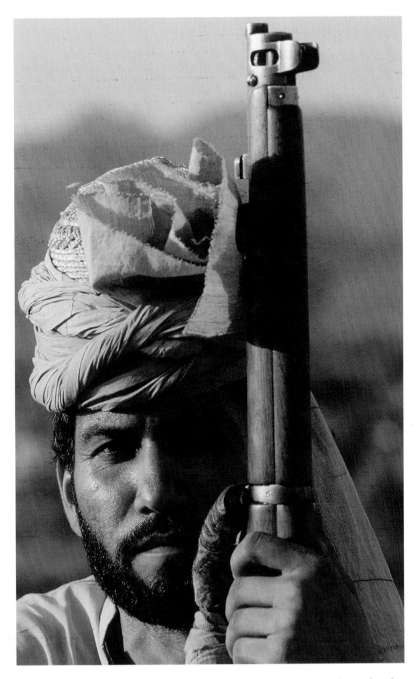

The Pashtuns are, in many ways, a violent people. Their strict code of honor requires them to seek revenge for any slight. This man from the northwest frontier is a Pashtun, or Pathan.

The Baluchi

The second largest tribal group in Pakistan is the Baluchi, who live in the arid areas of Baluchistan, in southwest and central-west Pakistan. The Baluchi are probably of Turco-Iranian descent, and they have good relations with their relatives on the Iranian side of the border. For centuries, the Baluchi have managed to live in semi-independence, because theirs is one of the most barren landscapes on Earth. There are occasional oases, but Baluchistan stretches for hundreds of miles across salty deserts that intimidate most travelers. Images taken from space show that Baluchistan suffers from numerous sandstorms created by winds that come from the Arabian Sea and kick up dust overland. Only the hardiest people can live here, and the Baluchi are legendary for their endurance, good humor, and hospitality. A poem from Muhammad Iqbal, "An Old Baluchi to his Son," shows the love of the Baluchi for their landscape:

> Winds of these wastelands be your love! Bokhara,
> Delhi, are worth no more. Like running water
> Go where they will: these desert plains are ours, and
> Ours are these valleys.

Few Westerners spend any time in Baluchistan, but those who have report a Baluchi ritual called *hal*. When two Baluchi meet after a length of time, they are required to tell each other everything that has happened since their last meeting. The ritual is taken quite seriously, and sometimes the conversation lasts for hours. Nothing is allowed to be passed over. The few foreigners who wish to marry into the Baluchi tribe often bemoan the number of intimate details they must relate to their new countrymen.

The Baluchi are first-rate horsemen and nomadic herders. They move their flocks from south to north during the summer months, and then reverse the process during the winter.

The Baluchi are a hardy people who have adapted to survive in the harsh landscape of Pakistan's huge salty deserts. Today's Baluchi maintain many of the same traditions that were practiced by their ancestors, such as the men seen here.

The Mohajir

A group that is identified by status rather than tribe is the *Mohajir*, which means "refugee." At the time of the partition in 1947, hundreds of thousands of immigrants crossed the border from India to Pakistan. Most of them settled in Sind, where they are known as Mohajir. Many of them came with upper-class educations and professional skills, and as a result, the Mohajir have displaced many native Sindhis from positions of prominence. This has led to a degree of enmity against the Mohajir. The last few decades have witnessed occasional outbreaks of violence against the newcomers. Tension is highest in Karachi, where the Mohajir make up perhaps two-thirds of the city's population.

Other Ethnic Groups

After the Punjabis, Sindhis, Pashtuns, and Mohajir, there are a number of much smaller ethnic groups in Pakistan. One is the Brahui of central Baluchistan. Differences between Brahui and Baluchi are not immediately apparent to an outsider, but the two peoples do not mix. The Brahui claim to be direct descendants of the Prophet Muhammad. Linguistically and physically, however, they appear instead to be descendants of the original inhabitants of the Indus River valley, prior to the Aryan invasions.

Another small group are the Kalasha, also known as the Kafirs (nonbelievers), and sometimes as the Nuri. The Kalasha live in a handful of mountain villages on the border between Afghanistan and Pakistan, in the extreme northern part of the Northwest Frontier Province. The Kalasha are apparently not related to the Pashtuns, or to any other ethnic groups in the area. Until about 1900, the Kalasha were most distinctive for being non-Muslims in an area that was heavily Islamic in its composition. Many Kalasha were forced to convert by the emir (leader) of Afghanistan after the turn of the twentieth century, but the converted and non-converted members of the tribe seem to live peacefully together. Their principal town is Kamdesh.

Not all tribal groups have the full rights of citizens, and not all of them want those rights. Northern tribespeople live in semiautonomous areas that are not part of the commonwealth. They are administered by an agency that reports directly to the federal government in Islamabad.

Pakistan contains a great variety of peoples. This is largely because of the many invasions and conquests that have occurred over the centuries, but trade also has played an important part. From the time of Mohenjo-daro and Harappa, people have moved up and down the Indus River, across the Punjab, through the Khyber Pass, and into Afghanistan. The northern mountain areas have been more secluded, less influenced by passing conquerors and merchants. Even there, however, different villages and clans sometimes display an astounding variety of customs and attitudes.

Given the great diversity that exists among the peoples of Pakistan, it makes sense to follow the sentiments of the horse-trader in the novel *Kim*, that the faiths and peoples are like horses: They all have merit in their own region.

Although Pakistan is a young nation with a modern democratic government, unrest often threatens the country's stability. The capital of Islamabad was designed to protect the government during periods of civil disturbances.

CHAPTER

5

A Muslim Nation: The Islamic Republic of Pakistan

Among Muslims, Saladin's name is synonymous with courage, compassion, integrity and respect for culture.

—Akbar S. Ahmed, in *Jinnah, Pakistan and Islamic Identity: The Search for Saladin*

S aladin was a twelfth-century Kurdish general who led Muslim armies against the Christian European crusaders. He recaptured the city of Jerusalem in 1187, and allowed the Christians there to be ransomed by their relatives in Europe. This humane approach to conquest differed greatly from the brutal massacre carried out by the crusaders when they captured the city in 1099. For this and other reasons, Saladin remains one of the great heroes of Islam. It is natural that Pakistanis—and other Muslims around the world—would look for his modern-day equivalent.

The great Muslim leader Saladin took back Jerusalem from the European crusaders. Considered a hero by Muslims around the world, he has become a symbol of the kind of leader Pakistan needs today.

Pakistan became a nation on August 15, 1947. It is one of a handful of states that were born in the immediate aftermath of World War II: India, Israel, East and West Germany are other members of that group. Pakistan may be a very young country, but its roots are deep in the cross currents of south Asia and the Middle East.

Muhammad ali-Jinnah

Young nations naturally search for heroes. England looks to King Alfred; Russia looks to Peter the Great; and the United

States had a ready-made first leader in George Washington. Pakistan likewise had a hero ready the day it became a nation. His name was Muhammad ali-Jinnah.

Jinnah was born in Karachi in 1876. His parents were comfortable, middle-class Muslims, and he grew up in an environment that recalled the earlier, glorious days of Muslim unity. The late nineteenth century was not a good time for Muslims around the world. They saw their once-great countries and empires fall into the hands of foreigners (mostly the British), and the Arab Muslim world had fallen far behind the West, particularly in the area of military technology. Jinnah was one of a number of twentieth-century Muslim leaders who would work hard to reverse this trend. He would meet with considerable, though long-delayed success.

Jinnah went to London as a young man and studied law at Lincoln's Inn. He became a barrister (lawyer) by the age of 20, and when he returned to Karachi, he was practically the only Muslim attorney in what is now Pakistan. Handsome, impeccably dressed, and often haughty with strangers, Jinnah became a familiar face to the British government and to fellow Muslim leaders on the subcontinent.

Like most people, Jinnah was not as one-sided as he often appeared. Although he spent his life working for a nation that would separate the Muslims from the Hindus, Jinnah married a Parsee (Zoroastrian). This aspect of his life is virtually off-limits for anyone conversing with a Pakistani today. Pakistanis remain mystified that their greatest leader could have married outside their faith.

Jinnah's relations with Mohandas "Mahatma" Gandhi remain somewhat mysterious. Several photographs seem to show that the two men liked and trusted each other, but there are also indications that each distrusted the power and influence of the other. The two leaders could not have been more different. Jinnah was elegant and urbane; Gandhi was purposely "dressed down" and identified with the poorer elements of Indian society. Despite their personal differences, Jinnah and Gandhi were two of the four men who determined the future of the subcontinent at the time of partition. The other two were Jawaharlal Nehru and Lord Louis Mountbatten, the last British viceroy (governor).

By early 1947, Jinnah was at odds with the other three men. Gandhi and Nehru wanted a united India—one flag for the entire subcontinent. Jinnah believed that he and his fellow Muslims would be oppressed by Hindu rule. Desperate to keep the subcontinent together, Gandhi and Mountbatten offered Jinnah a handsome bribe: to be the first Prime Minister of a united India. Jinnah refused. His stubbornness led to the partition of the subcontinent between India and Pakistan in August 1947.

Few people at that time knew that Jinnah was dying. He was suffering from tuberculosis and the strain of two decades as the leader of the Muslim movement. Despite his arrogant demeanor, Jinnah was a sensitive man who suffered from the criticism he received. He died on September 11, 1948, just one year after his dream of a Pakistani nation had come true.

Jinnah's death made him an instant hero to the Pakistanis. Even today he has no rival. He was and is the *Quaid-i-Azam* ("Great Leader"). Many people throughout the Middle East consider Jinnah one of the great Muslim leaders of all time. Some equate him with Saladin, the warrior-king who fought against the crusaders and who won Jerusalem for the Muslims.

Pakistan After the Partition

With Jinnah's passing, Pakistan settled into a more secure but less joyful time. There were numerous pressing problems. First was Pakistan's relationship with India. Second was the division between East Pakistan, centered on the Ganges River and the Bay of Benghal, and West Pakistan, centered on the Indus River and the Arabian Sea. The two problems fed into each other, since 1,000 miles (1,609 kilometers) of Indian soil lay between East and West Pakistan. Almost from the start,

Muhammad ali-Jinnah was the leader of the movement that demanded a separate nation for the Muslim people of the Indian subcontinent. Although he died in 1948, he remains the most respected leader in Pakistan's short history as a nation.

there were critics who claimed Pakistan was based on a flawed concept and could not endure.

The 1950s nearly proved the critics right. Tensions continued between Pakistan and India, and East and West Pakistan had serious strains in their relationship. Since the only strongly uniting factor was religion, Pakistan changed its name and approach to government in 1956. Its new title was the Islamic Republic of Pakistan.

To the credit of the government, there was no organized system against minorities in Pakistan. The official policy was toleration, but even so, minority communities stayed the same or shrank in size as the Muslim population increased by leaps and bounds. When Pakistan was formed in 1947, Muslims made up about 80 percent of the population; by 2000, they comprised 97 percent of the total.

No leader of Jinnah's stature emerged during the 1950s. Pakistan seemed to be stagnant in many ways. Meanwhile, India became more powerful, both in terms of population and in military strength, and Pakistan became concerned about its dangerous neighbor.

The 1960s were, on the whole, positive for Pakistan. Relations with India improved modestly, and Pakistan made important moves forward in irrigation, building the Tarbela Dam, and bringing electricity to many parts of the country. Military leader General Ayub Khan inspired a good deal of confidence.

If there was one burning issue that was often swept under the rug, it was population growth. Pakistan went from about 70 million to 100 million people between 1950 and 1980, and the explosion was particularly felt in urban areas. Karachi, which had been a quiet city of half a million people in 1945, suddenly became an urban jungle with nearly 10 million residents in 1980, and perhaps as many as 14 million by the year 2000. As quickly as Pakistan worked to irrigate the deserts and increase food production, the population bomb continued to tick, louder and louder.

Then came the beginning of the 1970s, and almost immediately, Pakistan was thrown into crisis. The divided state, located at the two wings of the subcontinent, was torn in two, and India took advantage of the situation to defeat the Pakistani army.

The 1971 War and Bangladesh

Tensions had existed between East and West Pakistan for some time. The two sections were about as different as could be. Hot, tropical, and densely populated East Pakistan resented the level of governmental control that came first from Karachi and then from Islamabad. West Pakistan, half desert and half irrigated land, could not identify with its eastern counterpart, which seemed too far away and different. The came the tragedy of 1971.

It was a time of conflict around the globe. The Vietnam War was still going on, although the United States was withdrawing its troops. The Arab-Israeli conflict was simmering, and would break into yet another war in October 1973. The "time of troubles" had begun in Northern Ireland about two years before. The Cold War between the capitalist United States and Communist Soviet Union was ongoing. Now, added to all this, came a war between Pakistan and India.

The 1971 war laid to rest the idea that the Muslims of Pakistan were natural soldiers and the Hindus of India natural cowards. India won most of the battles, and took about 100,000 Pakistanis prisoner. These prisoners of war languished in Indian jails for some time. Even worse, though, was the loss of East Pakistan. In the midst of the war with India, East Pakistan announced that it intended to be its own sovereign nation, separate from West Pakistan. Although there were attempts to change this course, both by force and by negotiation, the die was cast in the autumn of 1971, and what had been East Pakistan became the new nation of Bangladesh.

It was a grim time for Pakistanis. They hunkered down and determined to wait for the situation to get better. To a large extent, the next 20 years brought only more of the same: poverty, illiteracy, rapid population growth, and continued tensions with neighboring countries.

In the wake of the loss of East Pakistan, the reduced country wrote a new constitution. The Constitution of 1973 provides for a chief of state (President), a head of the government (Prime Minister), and a bicameral legislature (Parliament). Even more than earlier documents, the 1973 Constitution states that Pakistan is a Muslim nation and that Islam is the recognized faith of the Pakistani people.

The new constitution did not keep Pakistanis from what one author has called "the search for Saladin." As a young, insecure nation, Pakistan naturally gravitated to charismatic leaders who promised dramatic solutions to national problems. One such leader was Zulfikar Ali Bhutto; another was his charismatic daughter Benazir Bhutto.

Leadership of the Bhuttos

Lineage counts in Pakistan, and the Bhutto clan has been important in Sindhi politics for generations. They claim descent from the earliest Muslim invaders in the eighth century A.D. Zulfikar led the family, and became Prime Minister of Pakistan in 1974. He was slowly edged out by the military leader General Zia. Bhutto was put in prison in 1977, and executed in May 1979. In her autobiography, Benazir Bhutto recalled the event:

> I stood in a daze, not believing what had happened to my father, not wanting to. It was just not possible that Zulfikar Ali Bhutto, the first prime minister of Pakistan to be elected directly by the people, was dead. Where there had been repression under the generals who had ruled Pakistan since its birth in 1947, my father had been the first to bring democracy. Where the people had lived as they had for centuries at the mercy of their tribal chiefs and landlords, he had installed Pakistan's first Constitution to guarantee legal protection and civil rights.

General Zia proceeded to establish a full-scale military dictatorship. He is remembered fondly by many Pakistanis today, not for his methods, but because he was a pious Muslim who attempted to bring the country more fully into compliance with the dictates of Islam.

Because of economic aid from the United States, which was spurred by the Soviet invasion of neighboring Afghanistan, Pakistan enjoyed relative political stability in the mid-1980s.

Benazir Bhutto, whose father had been the leader of Pakistan, was elected Prime Minister of the nation in 1988, after her opponent, General Zia, was killed in a plane crash. Bhutto was the first woman to become the leader of a Muslim nation.

Pakistanis were looking forward to better times when Benazir Bhutto flew from London, England, to Lahore in 1986. She was welcomed by more than one million people, but it is difficult to say whether this outpouring of support was also a condemnation of Zia's government.

Benazir Bhutto ran her own election campaign for Prime Minister in 1988. It did not look promising; General Zia managed to have many of her supporters banned from the polls in advance. On August 17, 1988, however, Zia's plane crashed, and the general was killed. All of Pakistan looked to Benazir Bhutto, and on December 1, 1988, she became Prime Minister, and the first woman ever to lead a Muslim nation.

Benazir Bhutto made a promising beginning, but she never lived up to her image as a tireless and faithful public servant. During her two terms as Prime Minister (1988–1991 and 1993–1996) corruption increased within Pakistan's government. Bhutto also proved as unable to make any headway on the issue of Kashmir as any of the men who had preceded her in office.

Nuclear Tests and International Relations

Bhutto alternated as Prime Minister with Nawaz Sham, who served from 1990 to 1993, and then from 1997 to 1999. Under his leadership, Pakistan achieved a long-desired goal: the production of nuclear weapons. Coming at the same time as the announcement of India's nuclear success, the news had a sobering effect on leaders around the world.

Early in May 1998, India conducted seven nuclear tests, all of them in the Thar Desert, which borders Pakistan. Just two weeks later, Pakistan responded with five successful nuclear tests of its own. Suddenly, there was no mistaking the fact that the subcontinent now had two major powers, both of which had nuclear capability.

Both Indians and Pakistanis responded with great enthusiasm to the tests. There was—as one commentator put it—little else for either nation to cheer about. If this was true of India, it was even more true of Pakistan, because the 1990s had seen a gradual erosion of the economy and the faith of the Pakistani people in their government.

Pakistan had been propped up by economic and military support from the United States during the 1980s. As long as Soviet tanks and soldiers were stationed in neighboring Afghanistan, the United States increased its aid to Pakistan each year, and the economy enjoyed a moderate prosperity. Even supporters of General Zia acknowledged that he did not use this brief time of prosperity to remedy the social ills of Pakistan. Instead, the money was funneled to the military, and specifically, to the nuclear weapons program.

American economic aid dwindled after the Soviets left Afghanistan, and even more so after the collapse of the Soviet Union in 1991. Pakistan's one fairly constant ally was Communist China. Pakistani-American relations deteriorated even further after the nuclear tests of 1998. American diplomats blamed both India and Pakistan for the rise in tensions on the subcontinent, and withheld economic aid from both nations.

Given all the bad news they had received during the decade, Pakistanis were not surprised when a military coup took place in October 1999. General Pervez Musharraf, the army chief of staff, led the coup when he learned that he was about to be dismissed by the Prime Minister. Musharraf took power in a three-hour coup, then gave the news to the Pakistani people on television. Musharraf emphasized that he did not relish his new position, and intended to give it up by October 2002. In the meantime, however, he said he would attempt to deal with Pakistan's many social and economic ills. Then came the events of September 11, 2001.

Terrorism and Muslim Extremists

On September 11, 2001, Muslim extremists, many of them from Saudi Arabia and Egypt, hijacked four airplanes and crashed two of them into the World Trade Center in New York City. Another hit the Pentagon in Washington, D.C., and the fourth came down in the Pennsylvania countryside. Thousands of American civilians were killed and wounded, and the American economy received a sharp jolt.

U.S. President George W. Bush proposed a tough new international campaign against terrorists. In his first major speech on the issue, Bush emphasized that the United States would not discriminate between terrorists and the regimes or nations that aided them. This put Pakistan on the spot. There was no question of Pakistan supporting terrorism, but Pakistan was one of only three nations worldwide that recognized the Taliban regime in

President Pervez Musharraf faced criticism from many Muslim groups after he decided to support the United States in its war on terrorism after the September 11 attacks.

Afghanistan that harbored the September 11 terrorists. Within hours of Bush's speech, President Musharraf faced a dilemma: Would he cooperate with the United States, or try to remain neutral in the coming conflict?

Musharraf decided to support the United States. He announced that Pakistan would allow U.S. planes the right to fly over Pakistan, and he broke off diplomatic relations with the Taliban regime. As the United States began bombing Taliban strongholds, Musharraf stayed loyal to his American ally, despite increasing pressure from Islamic groups at home.

By the beginning of 2002, it appeared that Musharraf's gamble had paid some dividends. Economic aid from the United States flowed to Pakistan once more, and the country was hailed for its role in the international war against terror. At almost exactly the same time, however, tensions between India and Pakistan threatened to undo all that Musharraf had accomplished.

Problems with India

In the global climate that followed the September 11 attacks, India used the heightened anger over terrorism to focus attention on Pakistani groups in Kashmir. The Bush administration appeared more sympathetic to India than to Pakistan. As a result, Musharraf promised to round up and contain fundamentalist and terrorist groups inside Pakistan.

It was a victory for India and a humiliation for Musharraf. Even so, foreign observers praised the Pakistani president's moderation and steady purpose. If anyone could keep the lid on the very different elements within Pakistan, it seemed to be Musharraf. In his moderation and willingness to compromise, Musharraf showed some aspects of the type of leadership Muslims admire most: the leadership style of Saladin.

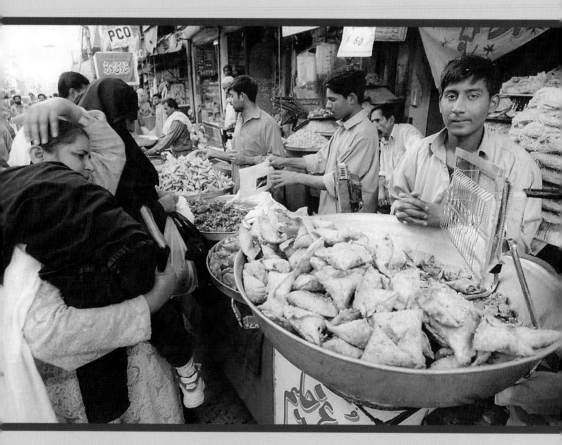

The Pakistani economy has had many ups and downs in the half century of the nation's history. Although the government struggles with problems of international trade and drug trafficking, most Pakistanis are more often involved in simple economic exchanges at local stores or food stands like this one.

6

Wheat, Cement, Opium, and Guns: The Many-Faceted Economy of Pakistan

In the 1980s the fall-out from the Soviet invasion of Afghanistan had created the "heroin and kalashnikov culture" that undermined Pakistan's politics and economy.

—Ahmed Rashid, in *Taliban: Militant Islam, Oil and Fundamentalism in Central Asia*

Pakistan is an upper-tier Third World country that aspires to join the ranks of the nations that boast developed economies. In the 55 years since independence and partition, Pakistan has made numerous forward strides, but they have all been at least equaled by the rise in population and demand for food. To make matters worse, in the 1990s, Pakistan developed a black market, or black economy, that amounted to more than one-third of the nation's total wealth. Opium production and heroin consumption threaten to undo much of the good that was achieved in the 1960s and 1980s.

Agriculture and Population Growth

Like all nations, Pakistan's economy can be broken down into three major components: agriculture, industry, and trade.

When independence was achieved in 1947, Pakistan was a thoroughly agricultural nation. Perhaps 80 percent of all Pakistanis were involved in the production or transportation of food. Today, that figure has dropped to between 50 and 55 percent, but there is little doubt that farming is still the backbone of Pakistani life. Without it, the nation would quickly become destitute.

The so-called Green Revolution came to Pakistan in the mid-1960s. American and European scientists extracted the fastest-growing seeds for wheat and rice and exported them to many nations of the Third World. Rice production soared in parts of Southeast Asia, and East Pakistan, which is now Bangladesh, was a recipient of that increase.

West Pakistan benefited both from the new cotton and wheat seed types, and from the importation of new farm machinery. Pakistan's food crops increased significantly during the 1960s and early 1970s. However, its overall population increased, as well.

Pakistan faces one of the problems encountered by most Third World nations: that of increased food production, better health care, and a soaring population. The first two factors are definite positives, in that people live healthier and longer lives. If the rate of births does not begin to decrease, though, Pakistan will head toward a population increase dangerously close to levels at which there will not be enough food for the people to eat. This has also been the case in India, Bangladesh, and many other Third World nations. Even Communist China, which rigorously controls its population growth, has expanded to become the largest society ever seen in human history.

The Issue of Irrigation

Wheat is the primary crop farmed throughout Pakistan. Irrigation projects along the Indus River and its tributaries have allowed for a great increase in the amount of arable land. Pakistanis now often farm in areas that their great-great-grandparents considered desert. This is a major improvement made through the system of irrigation set up by the British in the mid-nineteenth century, and continued by the modern nation of Pakistan. However, irrigation does have its critics and its flaws.

One of the major concerns is oversalinization of the land. When the land becomes overly saline (too salty) it slowly becomes useless. This might seem unlikely in Pakistan, where there is so much sand and desert, but there is a water table below the sand surface, and that water table has risen in recent years, clogging the arteries of farming land. Second, there is the problem of dislocation for farmers when major construction projects, dams in particular, have such importance.

The Indus River and its five tributaries have been dammed as much as possible. The result is that south of the Tarbela Dam, and especially in the province of Sind, the Indus no longer resembles the great river it was in previous days. Like the Colorado River between Arizona and California and the Columbia River in Washington and Oregon, the lower areas of the Indus flow with much reduced force.

The result of these dams is generally seen as positive. The dams allow for irrigation, which expands the amount of land that can be cultivated. But—and it is an enormous "but"—

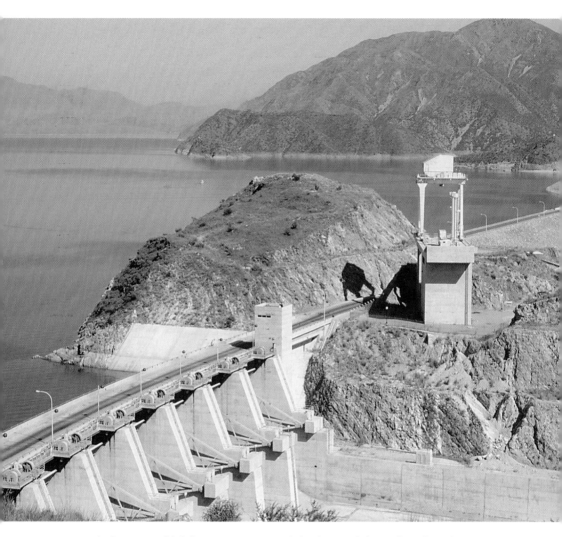

Tarbela Dam, which harnesses some of the force of the Indus River, is itself an impressive structure. It stands 486 feet (148 meters) high and is 8,999 feet (2,743 meters) long.

Pakistan faces the severe dangers of salinity in the soil and drought because its rivers no longer nourish the soil in the lower regions. If the level of salinity ever expanded to the point where much of the land in the Punjab became unfit for cultivation, Pakistan would be at the edge of complete famine and social collapse. A comment on the changing ideas about dams was offered by Indian scientist and activist Anuradgha Mittal:

> I was taught in school that India had become independent through a long struggle, and that if we wanted to maintain our independence, the country had to move forward with development: building dams, investing in high technology. I remember how, before movies, we'd see a newsreel about the prime minister christening a new dam, after which they'd play the national anthem. I would get tears in my eyes.

Though she writes about India, Mittal could just as well be talking about Pakistan or any other Third World nation. Later, Mittal came to a different conclusion about dams and their effect on Indian society:

> The dams were actually death centers that displaced millions from their lands with no restitution, and those in power didn't care about the thousands of people they dispossessed or killed. I suddenly realized that human beings have a great capacity for making decisions that intentionally starve others. I wanted to know why.

Whether one agrees with Mittal or not, most scientists and developers today recognize the dangers of building dams that change river flow and alter the lives of many people. Imagine if the United States did not have the Great Lakes and did not border the Atlantic and Pacific oceans. Imagine that 90 percent of the nation's water came from the Ohio, Mississippi, and Missouri rivers. Think of the consequences if those waters were to be dammed upstream, creating large reservoirs. It might help the growth of cities and industries, but millions of American farmers would have to either move or change their way of life. That is exactly what millions of Indians and Pakistanis have gone through for the past two generations.

Today, Pakistan holds its own in the agricultural sphere.

The country is self-sufficient in the staple crops of wheat, millet, and rice, and it even exports some wheat to other nations. However, Pakistan is built on an ecosystem that is stretched to its limit, and the continually increasing population may strain it even further in coming years.

Industry

Industry is the second cornerstone of economic development. Pakistan appeared woefully backward in industry when the country won independence in 1947. Just about the only industrial area in which the country was self-sufficient in that year was in the making of concrete, which has continued to be a moneymaker for the nation. British firms began the making of concrete in northern Pakistan in the 1920s, and the practice spread to the southern regions by the 1940s. Concrete remains one of the most important large-scale industries for the country.

Light industries have shown a much greater increase than heavy ones such as concrete throughout the 50 years since independence. Pakistanis have begun to make clothing in numerous small shops, many of which are labeled "sweatshops" by observers in developed industrial nations. Many of the clothes worn by Americans, Europeans, and Japanese are made in Pakistan.

Though it does not contribute to the balance of trade, gun making must be included among the major handicrafts and industries of Pakistan. An entire town 60 miles south of Peshawar makes its entire living from the production of guns. The gun makers there claim they can replicate any gun from anywhere in the world within one week of seeing the original. It is a Wild West town in which people who have made recent purchases empty rounds of ammunition into the air. This rowdy influence is deplored by many upper-class Pakistanis, especially in the south. They complain that "Kalashnikov culture" has been brought by the exiles from Afghanistan. There may be some truth in this, but guns have been a staple of

One of Pakistan's most successful industries is clothing manufacturing. Some critics condemn Pakistani production centers as sweatshops whose employees, including children, work under deplorable conditions. Whether or not this is the case, Pakistan produces a large amount of the clothing worn in Western nations.

the Pakistani economy and of the life of its tribal peoples since the first firearms appeared in the eighteenth century.

Firearms are more dramatic than poppy flowers, but the latter are at least as important to the black market in Pakistan. There are many types of poppy flowers around the world, many of which are not capable of producing an altered state in human beings. But *Papaversomniferum*, which is grown in

Pakistan and neighboring Afghanistan, is the substance of heroin and opium.

Opium and the Black Market

Poppy fields abound in the Northwest Province and in the northern areas of Pakistan, and many farmers make a good profit from the poppies that are made into opium. Raising the opium poppy was legal until 1979, when the new government led by General Zia cracked down and declared that the production and use of any stimulants was against Islamic law.

Until about 1995, the nation of Burma was the leading producer of opium. During the mid-1990s, Afghanistan surpassed Burma, raising and exporting 2,200–2,400 metric tons of opium per year. Opium sales were the main support for the Taliban regime in Afghanistan, and neighboring Pakistan, too, must take some blame in the matter.

Beginning in 1993, Pakistan's government cracked down on the production and sale of opium. The program was a considerable success. Farmers in the Northwest Frontier Province were trained to grow different crops, and opium production fell by about 90 percent. This dramatic success was balanced by a new problem, however: opium and heroin consumption.

The Taliban government in Afghanistan depended completely on the sales of opium. The Taliban sent great amounts of opium into and through Pakistan. Sections of the Baluchistan Desert, which once saw mostly camels bearing wool and cotton, now witness high-speed trucks carrying opium and heroin. The drugs are taken to the Mahkran coast and shipped to drug markets in the major cities of Europe and North America. High-level Pakistani officials have been caught transferring drugs. In 1986, an army major was caught bringing 220 kilograms (485 pounds) of high-grade heroin from Karachi to Peshawar. The street value of that heroin was about $600 million in U.S. currency—almost equivalent to the entire U.S. foreign aid package to Pakistan that year!

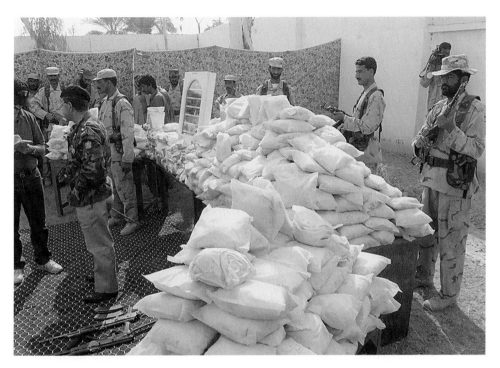

Although government efforts have successfully reduced drug sales, drug trafficking through and into Pakistan remains a serious problem. The officials in this photograph seized $550 million worth of heroin and morphine in January 2002.

Worst of all has been the increased drug use by Pakistanis. Government documents report that there were virtually no heroin addicts in Pakistan in 1979. The number of addicts rose to about 150,000 in 1985, and by 1999, the number had reached about 5 million people. If these figures are correct, it is safe to say that drug use, along with Islamic extremism, has become one of the major dangers facing the nation of Pakistan.

International Trade

Legal trade with foreign nations—as opposed to the illegal traffic in drugs—has been a major element of Pakistan's economy over the past 50 years, bringing in large sums. All these figures are in millions of rupees (Pakistani currency).

The nation's major trade partners are the United States (60,890); Hong Kong (20,654); Germany (18,929); the United Arab Emirates (14,421); and Japan (9,696). The major import nations are the United States (26,737); Japan (26,597); Saudi Arabia (21,825); Kuwait (17,487); the United Kingdom (14,395); and Germany (13,413).

Pakistan's trade suffered between 1996 and 2001 when the Taliban ruled Afghanistan. During that period, trade in illegal goods soared, while legal trade was stagnant or declined. The cost to Pakistan's economy has been estimated by Ahmed Rashid: "Industry and trade became increasingly financed by laundered drugs money and the black economy, which accounted for between 30 and 50 per cent of the total Pakistan economy."

Pakistanis Abroad

One final ingredient has to be added into the economic formula: Pakistanis who work abroad. Pakistan's economy was robust enough during the 1960s that most Pakistanis chose to stay home and work in the growing industries. After cutbacks in U.S. foreign aid during the 1970s, a boom in oil prices led many Pakistanis to move temporarily to Saudi Arabia, Kuwait, and the United Arab Emirates (U.A.E.) to work in the oil industry. Perhaps 2 million Pakistanis now live abroad in Arab nations, and as many as 5 million Pakistanis live in Europe and the United States. Even if they become citizens of the nations in which they live, most Pakistanis abroad retain a deep loyalty to their homeland, and the money they send back is definitely important to the economy of Pakistan.

In sum, Pakistan has a hybrid economy, one based on an almost equal division between agriculture, industry, and service industries. It is a fragile economy, both because of geographical considerations such as soil salinization and geopolitical factors such as the proximity of Afghanistan and conflicts over oil pipelines. What Pakistan's economy lacks most is coherent management. The Pakistanis are a hardworking, proud people who want to succeed in the capitalist world, but the landscape and environment they have inherited is better suited to a combination of a free-market with government management.

To the extent that any Third World nation can become a developed country, Pakistan has that opportunity. However, the country will remain on the verge of disaster as long as its population growth continues at the current rate.

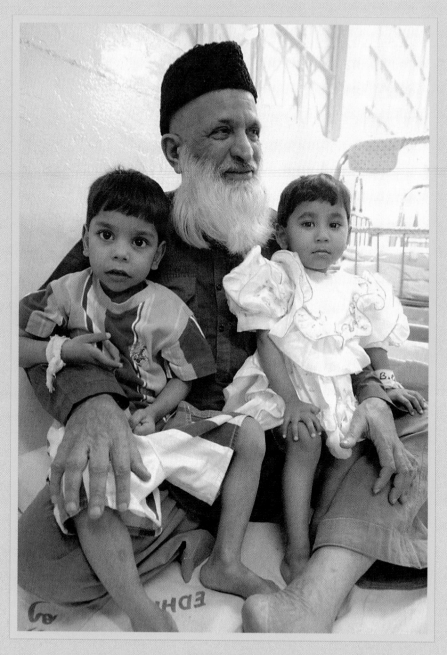

Famous humanitarian Abdul Sattar Edhi's efforts to improve society and protect children and the poor have won him the respect of his fellow Pakistanis, to whom he is a folk hero.

7

Living in Pakistan Today: A Study of Folk Heroes

Patriotic sentiments dictate that if you are one thing—a citizen of Pakistan, for instance, or a citizen of India—you cannot be the other. This sense of exclusivity and opposition has made it difficult for Pakistan to form its own distinct identity. There is no doubt in the minds of most Pakistanis that they are not Indians, but still the larger question, "Who am I?" remains unanswered.

—Stephen Alter, in *Amritsar to Lahore*

M any people in Pakistan today identify themselves first as Muslim, second as tribal or clan members, and third as Pakistani. This does not mean that Pakistanis are unpatriotic; far from it. Many Pakistanis fervently wave their flag and exclaim "*Hum hain Pakistani! Hum Jitengey! Hum Jitengey!*"

(We are Pakistani! We will win! We will win!). As Stephen Alter puts it, though, the question for them remains, "Who am I?"

All regional studies tend to come up with composite examples of what people's lives are like. Perhaps a better appreciation of what Pakistanis want from themselves and their nation can be gained from a study of people who are heroes to present-day Pakistanis.

The first hero of Pakistan was Muhammad ali-Jinnah, who died in 1948. Much as they revere Jinnah's memory, few Pakistanis today can remember much about him, since he died more than 50 years ago. No Pakistani leader since Jinnah has evoked the same type of admiration; even the Bhuttos had as many critics as they had fans. Therefore, Pakistanis have found a series of folk heroes, who give some idea of what it means to be Pakistani.

Abdul Sattar Edhi

Religious beliefs require Muslims to give charity to the poor. The recognized amount is 2.5 percent of a person's yearly income. Some Pakistanis go much further: They are leaders of humanitarian efforts.

Abdul Sattar Edhi is one of the most instantly recognizable heroes of Pakistan. Born in Gujarat in 1931, Edhi spent years of his youth caring for his mother, who suffered both from paralysis and mental illness. He moved to Pakistan at the time of the partition. He set up a free medical treatment center and a trust fund to support an ambulance service.

That was only the beginning. Edhi went on to create 13 free homes for unwanted or abandoned babies. About 6,000 people live in these homes today. He also developed a train and a fleet of ambulances and rescue vehicles that are known for their prompt responses to accidents. There are also animal shelters and a pilot program of posts for the aid of accident victims along Pakistan's highways. All this and more has been funded by the will, determination, and compassion of one man: Abdul Sattar Edhi.

Imran Khan

A second folk hero, of a very different type, is Imran Khan. Born in 1952, Khan attended school in Lahore, then went to England to study at Oxford's Keble College. There, he became a star cricket player, serving as Oxford's team captain in 1974. Khan then returned to Pakistan and became captain of the national cricket team. He served between 1982–1983, 1985–1987, and 1988–1992. In that final glorious year, Khan led the team to victory over the British in the World Cup finals held in Melbourne, Australia.

Khan was a household name in Pakistan for the rest of the decade. Known as the world's most eligible bachelor, he remained a playboy until 1995 when he married Jemima Goldsmith, daughter of a British multimillionaire. Jemima converted to Islam and took the new name "Haiqa." Jemima adapted to Pakistani life, wearing traditional clothing and becoming actively involved in charity work. She and Khan have two children and live in Lahore.

Soon after his retirement from cricket in 1992, Khan experienced a personal return to Islam. Rejoicing in his newfound faith, Khan decided to enter politics. Pakistani disillusionment with the government had reached an all-time high in the mid- and late-1990s. The reforms promised by Benazir Bhutto had not come about, and Pakistanis felt that in many ways, they were worse off than they had been a generation before. Khan formed a new party, the *Tehrik-e-Insaaf*, and announced his candidacy for Prime Minister. He ran a spirited, though flawed campaign. Khan got off to a bad start when an American woman accused him of fathering her four-year-old daughter, a charge Khan denied. For a few weeks in January 1997, the overseas Pakistani press, especially the six Bengali-language newspapers in New York City, had a field day with the rumors and speculations.

Khan continued his campaign, but lost in the February election. He and his followers did not win a single seat in

Imran Khan, who became famous for his skills as a professional cricket player, ran for Prime Minister of Pakistan in 1997. He campaigned on a promise to clean up the corruption that was prevalent in Benazir Bhutto's administration. Although he had many supporters, he lost the election.

Parliament (the legislature). Khan may have failed in part because Pakistani election law allows the right to vote only after age 21. Many of his admirers were much younger.

Nusrat Fateh Ali Khan

A third folk hero, perhaps the best-known Pakistani of the last 20 years, is Nusrat Fateh Ali Khan. Born in Faisalbad in 1948, Khan came from a family that had provided *qawwali* singers for over 600 years. Qawwali are devotional songs, based on poetry.

Khan originally intended to become a physician, but he eavesdropped on his father's singing classes and then studied with him. Khan's first public performance was at his father's funeral in 1964. He then sang with his father's two brothers, and after the death of one of his uncles in 1971, he became the leader of the family. His fame spread throughout Pakistan during the 1970s, and then throughout the world in the following decade.

He first performed in England in 1985, where he formed an important friendship with rock singer Peter Gabriel. The two men collaborated on the soundtrack to the controversial film *The Last Temptation of Christ* in 1988. Peter Gabriel's label began to produce albums of Khan's singing.

Khan's health began to fail in the 1990s. Like many Western opera singers, he was extremely overweight and suffered from liver problems. Nevertheless, he continued to perform to sold-out audiences at New York's Radio City Music Hall as late as 1996. Khan died in 1997, leaving millions of fans from around the world stunned. His nephew, Rahat Nusrat Fateh Ali Khan, became his successor. He has already performed around the world, including at the Hollywood Bowl and in New York City's Central Park.

Muhammad Abdur Rahman Chughtai

Muhammad Abdur Rahman Chughtai was a fourth important Pakistani folk hero. Born in Lahore in 1889, Chughtai started his education at a mosque (Muslim house of worship) in Lahore, then went on to study art at home and abroad.

Chughtai was steeped in Mughal and Muslim tradition, but he looked to the West for some of his inspiration. Watercolors and etchings were known in Pakistan only as imported art forms until Chughtai began to mold them into styles that honored earlier Mughal works. Perhaps most important, Chughtai introduced portraiture to Pakistan. Muslims believe that any direct representation of the Prophet Muhammad or of Allah are idolatry, and portrait painting never flourished until Chughtai's work became known. He made portraiture respectable in Pakistan.

Pakistanis are most familiar with Chughtai's engravings, but his watercolors are better known abroad. It is said that British Queen Elizabeth II has eight Chughtai watercolors in her private collection. Other Chughtai works have been part of numerous exhibitions outside of Pakistan.

Chughtai died at his birthplace in Lahore in 1975. His son completed a new museum of his father's works in 2000.

The Role of Women

No women are included in this list of Pakistani folk heroes. This is not meant to suggest that there are no heroines in modern-day Pakistan. Rather, the lack of women suggests that since the late 1970s, when General Zia proclaimed a return to traditional Islamic law, women have been increasingly cloistered in Pakistani society. Women are expected to play a secondary, supporting role to their husbands. The distinction between the sexes, drawn at birth, was described by journalist Jan Goodwin:

> The delivery of a baby boy is greeted with felicitations, parties, and, in some Muslim countries, even celebratory bursts of gunfire. The birth of a girl, on the other hand, is invariably a time for mourning. Even in everyday speech in much of the Arab world, when a silence falls at a gathering, the phrase uttered is Yat Bint, 'a girl is born.' And when one is, midwives have been known to abandon a delivery the moment they realize the child they have just helped into the world is of the "wrong" sex.

In Pakistan, and in much of the Third World, the birth of a girl is seen as bad fortune because she will eventually leave her family home and become part of the "wealth" of her husband's family. Because of this perceived loss, many Pakistani families do much less for female children than male ones. Boys and girls receive different treatment in everything from schooling to clothing, and even to food.

There was a period, between about 1960 and 1980, when young Pakistani women were given more opportunities for growth and advancement. Many middle-aged women in Pakistan remember this as a time of glorious possibility. For nearly all women born after 1980, however, the future seems grim. Pakistan has reverted to a traditional, fundamentalist code for the genders.

The Pakistani People

As this short list of folk heroes suggests, Pakistanis are an enthusiastic and emotional people. Although the British Raj endured for just over a century, it left some important imprints on Pakistan. This can be seen in the excitement over sports such as cricket and the desire to send musical geniuses such as Khan abroad to win international recognition. Pakistanis are talkative people, who often ask questions that some outsiders find embarrassing. Writer Stephen Alter recounted several episodes in which he was bombarded with questions before he even got to know the questioner. One of these conversations indicated both the eager nature of Pakistani questions and how much they know about American culture:

> Immediately I saw a young boy running toward me. He was eight or nine years old and grabbed my hand in excitement.
> "Are you American?" he asked, in Urdu.
> When I nodded he seemed delighted.
> "Then you must have seen a farishta," he said. "Tell me what they're like."
> Farishta is the word for angel, but his question still puzzled me.
> "What do you mean?" I asked.
> "You know, the farishta you have in your country," said the boy, insistently,. "Haven't you seen them?"
> By this time five or six other children had gathered around me, all of them about the same age.
> "I'm sorry, I don't know what you mean," I said. "What kind of farishta?"
> The boy and his friends looked up at me impatiently. "You know, the ones we see on TV."

The children then struck a pose that showed Alter they were referring to the superheroes of an American show. Even a country such as Pakistan, which prides itself on being the largest and most cohesive Muslim nation in the world, is not immune to the attractions of American music and television programs.

Pakistan today is steeped in Islamic tradition yet determined to become a more developed industrial nation.

8

Pakistan Looks Ahead

Two planets meeting face to face.
One to the other cried "How sweet
If endlessly we might embrace,
And here for ever stay! how sweet
If Heaven a little might relent,
And leave our light in one light blent!"
But through that longing to dissolve
In one, the parting summons sounded.
Immutably the stars revolve,
By changeless orbits each is bounded;
Eternal union is a dream,
And severance the world's law supreme.

—Muhammad Iqbal, "Two Planets."

It is impossible to say whether Muhammad Iqbal's poem referred to the time-honored tradition of star-crossed lovers, to the law of physics, or to the factors that separate nations and peoples from one another. Perhaps he meant all of the above in his poem, "Two Planets."

If Iqbal's poem is interpreted in a geopolitical manner, then it might be said that he was a prophet as well as a poet. This poem could be used to describe the dilemmas faced by Pakistan and India in the twentieth and twenty-first centuries.

Iqbal's poem brings to mind the many factors that lead toward separation and disunion within Pakistan. Iqbal died in 1938, but even now, in the early years of the twenty-first century, the kind of questions he asked are still relevant: Will Pakistan endure? Will its people be content? Will the pressing problems of population growth and poverty be overcome?

The dangers that Pakistan confronts are numerous. Population growth remains the main dilemma. Karachi has become one the of world's largest cities, with more than its share of drugs, poverty, and crime. The division between rich and poor continues to grow. Then, looming above all the other problems, is the seemingly unsolvable conflict with India.

Whether the tensions could be ended if the two nations came to an agreement over Kashmir is uncertain. The Indian-Pakistani conflict is a very deep one, rooted in the migration of Hindus to India and Muslims to Pakistan in 1947. These moves left millions of people uprooted. Numerous people on both sides of the border have never met their relatives on the other side. This division by borders might be overcome if there were goodwill between the two governments, but such goodwill does not exist. In fact, some journalists believe the two governments actually fuel the border tensions in order to control dissent in their home populations. Whether or not this is true, there is no doubt the situation has grown more serious since May 1998 when both nations tested nuclear devices.

The situation is unlike the Cold War that was waged

Although tensions have run high ever since India and Pakistan were created in 1947, the conflict has escalated over the years. Now that both nations have nuclear weapons, the problems between them pose a threat to the entire world. These Pakistani villagers near Lahore in Punjab are fleeing from the border area because of the India-Pakistan conflict.

between the United States and Soviet Union in the second half of the twentieth century. The two superpowers did not share borders, except for some icy islands in the Bering Strait. Even though their rivalry was intense and worldwide, there was no religious dimension to their conflict. By contrast, Pakistan and India have a feud that is economic, political, and religious.

Recent studies estimate that at least 100 million people would die on the two sides combined if there were a nuclear exchange on the subcontinent. That would only be from the explosion of bombs. The fallout that would ensue would also poison the environment of hundreds of millions of other people. For these reasons, a nuclear exchange must be prevented.

History tells us that a people and a nation cannot endure if they are split apart from each other. It may, therefore, have been a blessing in disguise when East Pakistan went its own way in 1971 to become Bangladesh. By doing so, Bangladesh paved the way for West Pakistan to become a more unified nation-state.

Geography tells us that centripetal and centrifugal forces are constantly at odds in nation-states. This can be seen in the United States. Although the Civil War (1861–1865) ended most attempts at outright separation, there are many aspects of American life that still divide people. The geographer and sociologist Garreau claimed in 1980 that there were nine nations of North America, not one. Garreau identified the following "nations": Quebec, New England, the Foundry, Dixie, Mexamerica, Ectopia, the Islands, the Empty Quarter, and the Breadbasket.

The history of religion demonstrates that spiritual leaders and different faiths have thrived on the Indian subcontinent. Religious plurality, rather than religious oneness, has been the norm in south Asia, but it is uncertain whether religious plurality will return to Pakistan. Today, it is the land of the pure, a land for Muslims in a sea of Hindus and Christians.

The history of politics suggests that Pakistan has a rough road ahead. The very concept of the nation-state is in some trouble in the twenty-first century. Inventions such as the Internet, cellular phones, and other means of communication have the potential to undermine the fierce adherence to nationalism of the nineteenth and early twentieth centuries. For a country such as the United States—which has practiced democracy for 200 years—or for one like Iceland—which has a remarkably homogeneous population—the twenty-first century may not be so threatening. For a nation such as Pakistan, however, born in 1947, and developed amid strife and conflict, it is possible that the system so painfully built by Muhammad ali-Jinnah could easily come apart.

This is especially possible in Pakistan because of the long-held tendency toward tribalism. The Pashtuns, for example, live as independently as possible from the national government, and have as much affinity with their fellow Pashtuns on the Afghan side of the border as with other Pakistanis.

This, however, does not mean Pakistan cannot survive. Pakistan may defy the odds and endure. It may even thrive. All that can be said with certainty is that the nation has surmounted many challenges in the last 50 years, and that it will likely face many more in the future.

Facts at a Glance

Land and People

Full Country Name	Islamic Republic of Pakistan
Historic Date	Formed in 1947 with the Partition of India and Pakistan
Area	310,527 square miles (803,943 square kilometers)
Population	135 million (1998 estimate)
Ethnic Groups	Punjabi, Sindhi, Pashtun, Baluchi, Mohajir
Religion(s)	Muslim (97%), Christian, Hindu, Parsee
Languages	Urdu (official), English, Punjabi, Sindhi, Pashtu
Capital	Islamabad
Major Cities	Karachi, Lahore, Rawalpindi, Faisalabad
Life Expectancy	Men, 63 years; women, 63 years

Economy

Major Products	Textiles, fetilizer, steel, chemicals, cement
Major Imports	Wheat, crude oil, machinery
Major Trade Partners	USA, Japan, United Kingdom, Saudi Arabia, Germany
Gross Domestic Product	$59 billion in 1998–1999
Currency	Pakistan Rupee
Average Annual Income	$441 in 1998–1999

Government

Form of Government Islamic Republic with President and bicameral Legislature. Constitutional Law was suspended in 1999 after the coup led by General Musharraf

Head of State General Pervez Musharraf

Voting Rights Universal suffrage beginning at age 21. Does not pertain to the semi-autonomous tribal groups

Political Subdivisions There are four provinces (Punjab, Sindh, Northwest Frontier Province, Baluchistan) and the Northern Areas and Federally Administered Tribal Areas

2500 B.C.	A civilization appears in the Indus River valley. It has a number of cities, notable for their sophisticated city planning and irrigation.
1700 B.C.	The Indus River cities disappear.
1600–600 B.C.	Known as the Aryan or Vedic period; the Aryans are a group of central Asian tribes that enter the subcontinent and come to dominate in Pakistan and northern India.
326 B.C.	Alexander the Great arrives on the Indus; in the Punjab he fights a battle against King Porus; the Greek army floats down the Indus River, then splits into two groups; one returns to Mesopotamia by sea; the other, under Alexander, marches across Baluchistan.
A.D. 711	A Muslim army invades Sind from the Arabian Sea; this is the beginning of the introduction of Islam to the subcontinent.
1526	Babur, a Turco-Mongol, invades the subcontinent and founds the Mughal Empire.
1526–1760	The Mughal Empire rules northern India and Pakistan.
1757	Englishman Robert Clive wins the Battle of Plassey; the interests of the East India Company become paramount on the subcontinent.
1857	The Great Indian Mutiny takes place; Great Britain subdues the Hindu Revolt with difficulty; India is placed under the direct rule of Queen Victoria, and the subcontinent is called the British Raj.
1869	Gandhi born in Porandar, India.
1876	Muhammad ali-Jinnah born in Karachi.
1877	Muhammad Iqbal born in Sialkot, Punjab.
1889	Muhammad Abdur Rahman Chughtai born in Lahore.
1933	At Cambridge, England, a group of students from India invents the word *Pakistan,* which is drawn from *P* (Punjab), *A* (Afghan), *K* (Kashmir), and *stan* (Baluchistan).
1939	A group of German mountain climbers set out for Nanga Parbat, in northern Pakistan; they are taken prisoner by the British at the beginning of World War II.

1947   Lord Mountbatten arrives as the last British viceroy.

1947   The British withdraw and the subcontinent is divided into two countries: Pakistan and India; Pakistan is further divided into East and West Pakistan.

1948   Muhammad ali-Jinnah dies.

1952   Imran Khan born in Lahore.

1953   Climbers reach the top both of Mount Everest and Nanga Parbat.

1956   The country is renamed the Islamic Republic of Pakistan.

1960   Pakistan and India sign the Indus Water Treaty.

1968   Work begins on the Tarbela Dam in northern Pakistan.

1971   East Pakistan breaks away and declares itself the new country of Bangladesh.

1973   A new Pakistani constitution is approved; it provides for a President, Prime Minister, and bicameral Parliament.

1977   Zulfikar Bhutto is put in prison.

1979   Zulfikar Bhutto is executed.

1979   Opium cultivation is prohibited.

1979   Soviet Union invades Afghanistan.

1980–1988   The Afghan resistance fighters are assisted by arms, ammunition and technical advice from many nations, including the United States and Pakistan.

1986   Benazir Bhutto comes home to Pakistan.

1988   Zia dies in a plane crash; Benazir Bhutto becomes Prime Minister.

1992   Pakistan wins the World Cup in soccer.

1997   Nusrat ali Khan dies.

1997   Imran Khan runs for Prime Minister.

1998   India and Pakistan explode their first nuclear bombs.

1999   General Pervez Musharraf seizes power in a three-hour coup; he appoints an eight-member National Security Council and suspends the Constitution until he sorts out Pakistan's economic problems.

2001   Under Musharraf, Pakistan aligns itself with the United States in the war on international terrorism.

Ahmed, Akbar S., and Ahmed Akbar. *Jinnah, Pakistan and Islamic Identity: The Search for Saladin*. Routledge, 1997.

Ganguly, Sumit. *Conflict Unending?: India-Pakistan Tensions Since 1947*. New York: Columbia University Press, 2002.

Goodwin, William. *Pakistan (Modern Nations of the World)*. San Diego: Lucent Books, 2002.

Haque, Jameel. *Pakistan (Countries of the World)*. Milwaukee: Gareth Stevens, 2002.

Jaffrelot, Christophe, ed. *Pakistan : Nationalism Without a Nation?* Zed Books, 2002.

Sheehan, Sean. *Pakistan (Cultures of the World)*. Benchmark Books, 1996.

Bibliography

Ahmad, Kazi S. *A Geography of Pakistan.* Oxford University Press, 1964.

Ahmed, Akbar S. J*innah, Pakistan and Islamic Identity: The Search for Saladin.* Routledge, 1997.

Alter, Stephen. *Amritsar to Lahore: A Journey Across the India-Pakistan Border.* University of Pennsylvania Press, 2001.

Bhutto, Benazir. *Daughter of Destiny.* Simon and Schuster, 1989.

Burton, Richard F. *Sindh And the Races that Inhabit the Valley of the Indus.* London, 1851.

Fairley, Jean. *The Lion River: The Indus.* The John Day Company, 1975.

Garreau, Joel. *The Nine Nations of North America.* Avon Books, 1981.

Goodwin, Jan. *Price of Honor: Muslim Women Lift the Veil of Silence on the Islamic World.* Plume-Penguin, 1994.

Husain, Ishrat. *Pakistan: The Economy of an Elitist State.* Oxford University Press, 1999.

Kiernan, V.G., trans. and ed. *Poems from Iqbal.* John Murray, London, 1955.

King, John, Bradley Mayhew ,and David St. Vincent. *Pakistan.* Lonely Planet Publications, 1998.

Kipling, Rudyard. *Kim.* Macmillan, 1901.

Kux, Dennis. *Pakistan: Flawed not Failed State.* The Foreign Policy Association, 2001.

Margolis, Eric S. *War at the Top of the World: The Struggle for Afghanistan, Kashmir, and Tibet.* Routledge, 2000.

Mittal, Anuradha. "On the True Cause of World Hunger," an interview by Derrick Jensen, *The Sun*, February 2002.

Ptolemy, Claudius. *The Geography*, trans. and ed. Edward Luther Stevenson. Dover Publications, 1991.

Ramana, M.V., and A. H. Nayyar. "India, Pakistan and the Bomb," *ScientificAmerican*, Vol. 285,number 6, December 2001: 72–83.

Rashid, Ahmed. *Taliban: Militant Islam, Oil and Fundamentalism in Central Asia.* Yale University Press, 2000.

Robertson, Sir George Scott, K.C.S.I. *The Kafirs of the Hindu-Kush.* London, 1900.

Toynbee, Arnold J. *Between Oxus and Jumnai.* Oxford University Press, 1961.

White, Peter T., and Steve Raymer. "The Poppy—For Good and Evil," *National Geographic.* February 1985: 143–188.

Index

Index

Picture Credits

About the Author

SAMUEL WILLARD CROMPTON is a historian and biographer who lives in western Massachusetts. He is the author or editor of 20 books on topics that range from spiritual leaders of the world to lighthouses and the American presidents. One of his most recent books, *Meet the Khan,* features the travel journals of three thirteenth-century Europeans who traveled east to meet three Mongolian Khans: Kuyuk, Mongke, and Kublai.

CHARLES F. "FRITZ" GRITZNER is Distinguished Professor of Geography at South Dakota State University. He is now in his fifth decade of college teaching and research. Much of his career work has focused on geographic education. Fritz has served as both president and executive director of the National Council for Geographic Education and has received the Council's George J. Miller Award for Distinguished Service.